THE TACTICAL SOFTWARE ENGINEER

GETTING TO LEVEL I

By Tom Nicholas

Dedication

*This book is dedicated to educators at all levels who go
beyond theory to teach their students reasoning and
practical application of their subject. When we are young,
we have little to no life experience to inspire us in the
classroom. Without exception, my favorite teachers and
professors were the ones with the courage to step outside
the box to engage us. From the English teacher who
pridefully dons medieval garb to pull us into the world of
Shakespeare to the one teaching the Science of Star Wars in
full Stormtrooper battle gear, you make the difference.
Thank you.*

Contents

PART I: FOR THOSE OF YOU ABOUT TO CODE, I SALUTE YOU

Why this book

When we are first born our parents look upon us with adoring eyes hoping we'll become smart, happy, strong, and caring adults. And as we grow, our confidence is built- we succeed in school, clubs, and even on sports teams. If you are one of those people who reject the head-banging of the school football team in favor of the more interesting piece of technology in front of you, then this book is probably for you.

Over the next ten to twenty years the evolution of technology will continue rapidly, creating millions of exciting and intellectually-challenging, high-paying careers. Future engineers will greatly benefit society in a myriad of areas including health care, defense, commerce, pure science, and more. *Would you like to become one of them?*

There is more than one way for a person starting at Level I, with little more than a dream, to become a professional engineer. I am about to walk you through the interesting, funny, and awkwardly crooked path of my becoming a technology professional. And I will do so with sincere hope you'll leverage these lessons and hit the ground running.

The Tactical Software Engineer: Getting To Level I is organized into five sections:

- *Welcome To Level I*: Here I discuss our high school years and the lessons learned in my first failed attempt at college.

- *Finding My Future*: In this section I take a deep dive in describing how serving a tour in the United States Navy helped me grow personally, discover my future with technology, and even set aside money for college.

- *Behold, The Green And Gold*: Ever wonder what it's like to see the shoe on the other foot? To be an economically-disadvantaged white student attending historically-black Norfolk State University? You'll want to get comfortable for this tale of cultural and intellectual immersion.

- *My Survey Of Today's Landscape*: Along with choosing a school and obtaining a foundational technical education, engineers need to have an understanding of the many job titles and roles of the people with whom they'll work. This section describes them.

- *Choosing Your First Company*: Upon graduation, you'll experience the excitement of working for your first company. **And yes, as an in-demand technology professional, you'll get to choose!** In this final section I cover thirty-three different topics worthy of your consideration when selecting that first position.

This book was written for students interested in a career in software engineering.

Let's get to it.

The Job Market

The job market for engineers, especially software engineers, is amazing for as far ahead as anyone can see. Combined, websites such as *Dice.com, Indeed.com, LinkedIn.com, and TheLadders.com* have many tens of thousands of openings constantly flowing into their databases. New companies are born, some expand operations, and others merge. All this activity creates such an excess of opportunity that each year large and medium-sized companies lobby congress to import foreign engineers to fill the gap. To the latter point, those engineers with solid development and people skills who are proactive and intellectually invested in their organization will always be in high demand. It's not uncommon for companies to charge their clients $300 US per hour for software engineering services. In a typical 2,000 hour year your efforts could represent $600,000 US worth of revenue generating awesomeness. That's the good news.

The less than good news is you aren't going to make even half that as a regular employee. However, you can easily and consistently earn a solid six-figure income, great benefits, in a comfortable environment, along with ample vacation time to enjoy the life you will have earned.

At this point, some folks might say, "He's all about the money. Life is much more than that." Indeed, a full life is much more than that. Fulfillment in life includes many components. One's career is just a single part of it. Career fulfillment itself has many aspects; intellectual, social, financial, and more. *Engineering skills are portable, meaning at will you can pick up and offer your services to companies and people more aligned with your interests, morality, and life goals any time you like.* And those preferences you'll discover will naturally evolve over time.

Early in your career you may be single, care-free, and interested in the excitement of the big city or perhaps you may choose a position that offers company-paid world travel. In your mid-career life there is a good chance you will be married with children of your own and a position with solid monetary output might become a higher priority. And in the twilight of your career you may come to feel the good you do and things you leave behind for future generations are what matter most.

The key ingredient throughout these life phases is your engineering skill set. It allows you to adjust your path at selected, discrete points in time. This option to move as you like is due to the law of supply and demand. There are far more cool engineering opportunities out there than people available to fill them. So you, my friend, will be in the driver's seat. Circling back to the point in this section's first paragraph, the need for good engineers is so strong companies continue to lobby the United States Congress to bring in foreign workers to lend a hand.

At the time of this writing, U.S. regulations limit the number of foreign nationals who may be issued a visa or otherwise provided H-1B status each fiscal year to 65,000. The law has written into it several kinds of exemptions that allow the import of even more workers. According to a recent Specialty Occupation Workers report to the U.S. Congress, the number of H-1B petitions approved that year was 262,569. Workers in computer related occupations comprised 61% of this number.

That's roughly 160,167 imported foreign high-tech workers- enough to overflow the nation's largest football stadium at the University Of Michigan all the way into the parking lot.

The need for those with engineering skills is so dire that Microsoft's Bill Gates and Steve Ballmer and Facebook's Mark Zuckerberg, among others, helped fund *Code.org*. They have been using the number of open computing jobs across America to convince parents and school districts to expand K-12 computer science offerings so they can help fill these positions. However, the process of educating quality engineers takes time. In parallel Mr. Gates and Mr. Zuckerberg also supported FWD.us, an organization invested in immigration reform that could make it easier for foreign engineers to migrate to the United States to pursue their dreams.

The advancement of knowledge and the betterment of the human condition for everyone is the bigger picture here. So it makes sense to pursue multiple strategies in making that happen.

More good news for you: If you are reading this in the English language there's a chance you're already in America. As a professional software engineer with more than twenty years' experience, let me invite you to one sweet pool party. The Sun is out, the water warm, and there's an open spot just for you.

PART II: WELCOME TO LEVEL I

Spheres Of Influence

If you are in your late teens or twenties you're really just getting started and have likely been receiving life and career advice from parents, aunts and uncles, clergy, teachers, coaches, and others. To this point I'm sure much of it has been great but some of it has surely left you scratching your head and wondering where they're getting this stuff.

The vast majority of the time, people base the advice they give you on *their* experiences, things *they've* heard or read, and *their* personal dreams and limitations- not yours. The decisions you take based upon the opinions of those around you is what I call your "sphere of influence." And understanding the world view of those offering you advice is critical to meaningful evaluation of those opinions.

The first time I gained insight into this truth was in my senior year of high school. You see, when I was an eighth grader I loved the game of football, was very athletic, and wanted to play quarterback. Each fall I attended high school varsity games with my parents. I also played at the freshmen and junior varsity high school levels. Hanging out with other boys, I mentioned to them my dream of playing quarterback. Unbeknownst to me a couple of them also wanted to play the position and told me in order to make it I'd have to throw the ball and hit a six-inch by six-inch handkerchief from seventy five yards away. That was too much for me to imagine. And the fear of not ever being able to achieve that skill-level kept me from trying out for the position at all. *Turned out, their opinions were totally inaccurate.* They couldn't do it and college and NFL players can't do it either. Years later, after having toiled away at football positions requiring a little less skill, it dawned on me that what they said were simply statements of their own limitations; not mine.

As I was growing up, my well-meaning parents said to me, "We want the best for you. We want you to be happy. You should go to college." On the one hand it was great to hear them express interest in my future. On the other they provided no specific motivation. Why college? Study what in college? To do exactly what after college? What did they mean by "be happy"? What does "happy" mean to a teenager without life experience? Ah, and then it dawned on me. Although I had lost four years not trying out for the quarterback position, they had lost decades by toiling away in basic occupations that didn't allow them to explore their own dreams. So it was hard for them to be more specific and to engender in me a faith in pursuing a precise career path beyond what they had done. To know what would fit me best, I needed to try some things to gain life experience. *As will you.*

As you explore possibilities and try new things your experiences will bring wisdom. And making adjustments to your life plan as you go will come more easily because those slight course corrections can be based upon your specific experiences. One of the things often on the minds of younger people is the fear they will fall behind their peers. *Let me tell you, although your education starts earlier, real life begins after high school and society doesn't care whether you find your career and happy place at twenty-two, thirty-two, or forty-two. The only thing that matters is that you keep trying until you do find it.*

Once you start down your path, you'll come to see there is no one more interesting, more magnetic, and more attractive than a person happily and passionately pursuing his dream. That having been written, the sphere of influence you choose when pursuing your dream definitely affects the result.

You need to be around people who are positive and encouraging- the glass-is-half-full types. They don't need to know everything you know about your dream but they do need to be supportive. If you find you've let someone into your inner circle that is persistently negative, then to protect your dream you've got to make the adjustment to back away from him. Plainly and simply, you have the right to pursue your dream.

So what are some important factors in choosing your dream? Here are a few:

- Will this dream help you grow intellectually, spiritually, or physically?

- Is it a short term goal or something you will be able to mentally and physically do over the long haul?

- Will you be able to financially support yourself while pursuing it and after achieving it?

- Does it benefit your community or society generally?

Why such a short list? If your dream helps you grow, is sustainable over the long haul, allows you to support yourself, and gives you satisfaction as it benefits others then the likelihood is good you'll end up a happy person.

If you feel the need for further permission then note this: On July 4th, 1776 our united thirteen states congress unanimously held some truths to be self-evident- that all of us are created equal and that we are endowed by our Creator with certain unalienable rights. It should be noted that this is equality under the law and these are legal rights, not physical or mental abilities. Therefore, the results of one's pursuit of his vision of the American Dream will vary based on his abilities. The great news is most of us can improve our chances of intellectually-based success with research, study, practice, and experience. I was not born with an aptitude for creating awesome user interfaces and software algorithms. In fact, when I was born the personal computer didn't even exist. It was invented when I was roughly sixteen years old and I didn't touch one for another eight years. That's when my engineering journey really began. If you are dreaming of a career in engineering today, let me offer encouragement. The realization of your dream awaits- you just need to apply yourself.

Two great quotes I've come to know are: "I'm a great believer in luck. The harder I work, the luckier I get." *–Coleman Cox, writer.* And, "It takes 20 years to become an overnight success." *–Eddie Cantor, American Performer.*

So how do these quotes apply? Almost no one is an overnight success and you'll need to apply yourself to achieve your vision of the American Dream. The best way to do this is to organize it into smaller achievable steps. How many? *As many as it takes.* Then take a moment to celebrate when you complete each step along the way. Your dream to become an engineer is waiting and if you dedicate yourself to it, you can realize it!

The High School Years - Learning About Yourself

While we matriculate through high school our minds and bodies are experiencing some incredible changes. Although one's physical evolution does affect his mental state, body changes are best discussed with parents and health class teachers so this book doesn't delve into them. On the mind front, high school provides the opportunity to develop significantly. Federal and state standards require students obtain essential knowledge and skills in areas such as English, Mathematics, Social Studies, Science, and more. These required classes certainly help build a great foundation. Beyond those are electives; classes students can choose themselves in helping them become more well-rounded and complete. Let's focus on non-computer, non-math-related ones as those two are obvious choices.

From my personal experience as a software engineer, some electives add more value than others. At the top of the list is typing skill. The more quickly one can accurately type, the more productive he will be. Typing is used in software development of course however it's also used in doing design work, responding to emails, taking meeting notes, and much more. Presuming you are either in America or headed here, I would next suggest courses in Español; the Spanish language. Look at the evolving demographics of North America. Consider the likelihood you will someday work with or for Latin American people. And even if you don't, who can resist the natural beauty and culture of Central and South America and the Caribbean when going on vacation?

When it comes to science electives, study all the way up to Physics if you can. Biology and Chemistry are fine and oftentimes required, however, software engineers do math. *Physics is applied mathematics!* Another great course to consider taking is Geography. Geography is the study of the physical features of the earth and its atmosphere, and of human activity as it affects and is affected by these, including the distribution of populations and resources, land use, and industries. Software engineers are often blessed with the opportunity to meet and work with people of different cultures. For example, I've worked with people from Australia, Bangladesh, Canada, China, England, Ireland, Israel, Italy, Russia, Siberia, and Ukraine. Studying geography is the first step in understanding other cultures and is a very helpful tool in building bridges of friendship. *Successful business relationships are built on friendship, understanding, and effective communication.*

Psychology is not a course usually offered at the high school level but understanding this too can prove to be useful. Absent a formal course, similar insights into human nature and what makes people think the way they do can be gleaned from, of all places, literature. While the books selected by teachers vary from district to district and school to school, the thought here is the same. Every story has a collection of characters that interact. Gaining the ability to understand those interactions and what drives them is a very useful skill in real life. *Successful software engineers master the ability to see things from the perspective of others and leverage that information in creating opportunities for success.*

Junior Recruit Officer Training or JROTC is a course of military training at the high school level that exposes students to the purpose, organization, life, and traditions within the United States Army, Navy, Marines, or Air Force. Participation in a high school unit builds self-discipline, teamwork, motivation, and confidence. Self-discipline is a skill critical to everyone pursuing a career in engineering because it leads to focus and attention to detail. Sloppily-written software tends to crash. Every software developer, as I describe later in this book, operates as part of a team and understanding the importance of functioning this way is critical to engineering success. *Through JROTC unit successes, confidence is built- and this confidence can motivate young students to passionately pursue their life goals and dreams.*

While I attended Middle Township High School, in Cape May Court House, New Jersey, I participated in our Navy JROTC unit for three years. During that time I made some life-long friends, enjoyed amazing visits to naval bases in Virginia, Maryland, Connecticut, and even went to sea for a week on an aircraft carrier off Pensacola, Florida. We participated in community parades, hosted and participated in drill meets, and served our local community in charitable ways as well. I highly recommend participation if your school has a unit.

Social Media And The Real World

One of the gauntlets you'll need to successfully run throughout your life, starting in your teen years, is the useless distraction known as social media. What you need to know up front about platforms such as Snapchat, Twitter, Facebook, and sites like this is they were created for exactly one reason- to make money for their creators. They do this by sapping every bit of nervous energy you have in luring you onto their rodent wheel of if-just-one-more-person-liked-you-life-would-be-awesome! Yeah, no.

Awesomeness in one's life happens when he interacts with the real world to positive ends. It doesn't happen through the sharing of dank memes, pet videos, or an endless trail of vain "look at me" selfies. Furthermore, what's happening behind the scenes is noteworthy and a little scary. These apps are vehicles to spam advertising in your face. If you don't believe me, try the following test:

Go onto Google, Bing, Yahoo, or any of them, and search for a product. Click into some big store that sells it. Now close all your browser windows. Next, log into your favorite social media website. Refresh the page and within seconds you are going to see ads for that thing you just searched.

These ads will follow you too- from site to site, search engine to search engine; tormenting you to buy. Every website you visit and everything you do and post is being tracked. And every bit of information you leave is being added to a profile on you that you will never see. However, this information is available to the highest bidder- people willing to buy it. But this is just half the equation.

Let's presume for the sake of argument all you do online is innocent, cute, and morally acceptable in society. A more important thing of yours, something definitely finite in nature, is being lost forever- your time. The time you spend on social media and in computer gaming is time you could utilize in planning and doing the awesome things you want to do with your life. As thought leader and author Seth Godin puts it, "What you are actually doing is hiding from the important things you could be doing." And the lure of social media, which includes gaming, is a very addictive and destructive drug for many people. When I was in the seventh and eighth grades, our school showed us movies of the side effects of drug abuse. Perhaps some school districts still show these or ones like it today. Similar, difficult to watch videos related to social media and gaming addiction are on YouTube. Search "parents destroying kid's electronics" and watch just a few. You will see the devastating effects abuse of technology can cause. These young adults have devolved into complete messes in desperate need of intervention. What has kept me on the right path is that I maintain a running to-do list, marking off what of it I will knock out in a given day. And this list is reasonably challenging. Once I've completed my tasks, I'm entitled to dabble just a little in fun online things. There's a pretty simple way to know if you're on the right track. If you are planning your life goals around your social media time, you've got a problem brewing.

Background media playing while you try to do your homework can seem a viable way to get through it but the truth is you do your best work with no distractions. Here's a second fun little test to try on two different nights where you have the reasonably-same amount of math homework. The first night, go ahead and put music or your favorite TV show on in the background. Write down the time and do the problems. Then write down the end time. On the second night, go to a room where there is complete quiet. Write down your start and end times there. Now compare the difference in total times. If the two sets of homework were reasonably similar in difficulty the likelihood is high you are going to notice a big difference- in the quiet session you were able to complete the homework more quickly and with fewer errors.

Celebrated science fiction author, Neil Gaiman, gets things done by making himself extremely bored. If he gets bored enough he entertains himself by getting done what's important to him. If you get bored enough you'll get your homework done.. and your house chores.. and the other things that add value to your family. Then you too will have a little time for whatever else. When that *earned* time comes, you'll be able to fully enjoy it because you won't have looming in the back of your mind the things you know you should have done first- the things that help you prepare for a bright future and make you a valued team player in your family and your life.

Friends For Life

Over the years through high school, college, time in the United States Navy, and through numerous jobs in companies, I was fortunate to have met a lot of interesting people. At virtually each point there has been a friend who became the kind I kept long term- the kind I didn't see or chat with for a year or more and when we did reconnect it's like we were only apart for a day. You too will come to build nice friendships that work this way- where you persistently build each other up and celebrate each other's successes. And these relationships are awesome.

Conversely, every so often I go back to my original home town, Cape May Court House, New Jersey, where I see friends and acquaintances who never left. Almost without exception, the people who never left relive a completely different kind of story each time we meet. And for them too, it's like we only saw each other yesterday. When we were younger, these ones who never left had big plans- they were going to do this or that *when the timing was just right.* Well guess what? The timing was never right and they now have a trail of excuses for why they didn't explore past the border of our little town. Truth be told, it wasn't about timing, it was about hiding from the great unknown that might affect their plans- unknowns that might lead to some kind of failure. Their fear of failure was so great they became paralyzed to the point they wouldn't even try. Well guess what?

Life is full of failure and as long as you aren't risking your life, you learn from it and you do get to try again. Without exception, the happy explorers I mentioned first definitely experienced failures in their lives. They lost jobs, totaled cars, had family issues of one kind or another, stopped and started school, got sick and then got better again. It happens to every single one of us. All of us who dared to venture out shared some traits. First, we had grit. Whenever adversity hit us, we took a tiny step back, analyzed what happened, made a new plan, and simply set out again. Secondly, we realized there was no such thing as a time machine. The past is the past and although we can learn from it, we couldn't change it. All we could do is keep moving forward.

When you bump into these positive-thinking, dedicated, fellow adventurer types, chat them up and offer encouragement. Strive to understand what drives them and how you might leverage their thinking and tactics too. You might just make a friend for life.

Attend College Right Away Or See The World?

Remember when you were younger and everything in the world seemed so big? You could barely see what was up on the kitchen counter, on the shelves, and on the playground you could barely make a basketball shot. Over the years you grew, could see everything in your house, and started making some of those basketball shots- or at least you doinked them off the rim. Now consider the size of the world. Really young kids have no concept just how big it is. High school students have been exposed to maps and watched movies that help them have some idea of it. Still, not having seen much of the world first-hand it's very difficult to appreciate the full geography of it. And it's impossible to leverage knowledge one doesn't have. The choices to attend college right away or see the world beforehand each have pros and cons. Let's compare and contrast some of them.

Attending College Right Away

Pros:

- A person earns a bachelor's degree by the age of twenty-two.

- Math skills are in-tact and not lost due to lack of use since high school.

- There is no commitment of time towards maintaining a marriage and having small kids for whom to care, and your parents are likely young enough they don't need your constant attention either.

- At this age, you are likely have a lot of free energy.

Cons:

- Energy one has can scatter almost uncontrollably. The excitement of being away from home for the first time, being around a lot of other students (especially the intellectually unfocused ones), access to mind altering substances, and limited supervision creates a difficult-to-avoid chaotic environment akin to an eight year old's birthday party two seconds after the piñata has split open. Yes, on the majority of American college campuses there are times that's exactly what it's like and these temptations can be overwhelming. There is a middle-ground though between being a monk and a member of a complete crazy college fraternity. This is something you'll need to carefully manage.

- Most things appear to be black and white and this especially applies to interactions with your professors- the way you look at your instructors and they you. The way you approach them about goals you have or questions about assignments is affected by the way in which you were raised and the amount of life experience you have in interacting with other people. And to get the desired results, tact and tactics matter. What follows is an example of what I mean.

  Consider a professor in a given semester, especially at a large university, could have four or five hundred students to track. The odds of you seeing him are dramatically low if you just walk into his office unannounced. The odds of getting that quality time increase significantly if you politely ask, "Is there is a good time for you when we could meet to discuss "Project X"? Some of you are saying, "But of course," and some are giving that Sheldon Cooperesque head-turn as if the law of gravity has been magically defied.

  The specificity of "Project X" is important. Hearing the reason, he'll know why you want to meet and can prep for it. His availability is limited given he may have a family, a life, may be tired, and that he sees many students. A typical engineering student coming straight from high school might not appreciate the helpful style in this request, however, someone who had experienced some of the world first likely would have.

- The last obvious consideration is money. You may just not have money for college and you may need to take out some significant loans to attend. Later in the book options for attending college with little or no money are discussed. Now let's consider the pros and cons of going the other seeing some of the world before attending college.

Experiencing Some Of The World First

Pros:

- Some my favorite college professors were ones who came to teaching later in life; after they had experienced something of the world. They were able to temper their teachings of theories with real-world experience. And something similar happens for students too.

  Meeting more types of people first-hand exposes us to different cultures and perspectives, and provides a glimpse into how the world really flows. Obtaining some of those insights prior to going in the classroom opens your eyes in wonderful ways and serves as a catalyst to natural curiosity. Upshot: you're going to enjoy college much more because you'll be able to relate your experiences to the things the professor is teaching.

  The value of marrying lessons from your past to what you're doing in a given moment carries on throughout your life and goes both ways. An interesting scene from the movie classic, Indiana Jones And The Last Crusade, comes to mind. Professor Henry Jones, Senior, is walking the beach after a narrow escape only to be confronted by a diving Nazi fighter plane. Holding nothing more than an umbrella, he finds a way to overcome these daunting odds by opening it and running towards a flock of seagulls that then fly up and take out the fighter plane. He says, "I suddenly remembered my Charlemagne: 'Let my armies be the rocks and the trees and the birds in the sky.'"

  That's applied knowledge. And it's the kind of thing that happens frequently in the real world when you marry practical experience with classroom knowledge. Well, except for being suddenly attacked by a Nazi fighter plane but you get the point. There is solid value in seeing a bit of the world before college.

- You may be able to save some money along the way. Serving in the military or taking on a public sector job helps build your confidence and is a great way to put away money for school. Through the U.S. Navy I was able to save enough for a few semesters of college, until my grades earned me a full academic scholarship. If you are willing to apply yourself, you'll be amazed at the number of people who are happy to help you succeed.

- You will learn more about yourself- the types of people, places, and things that interest you. This in turn will make selecting your college electives a lot of fun. Will you choose English Literature or Chinese Philosophy? Biomechanical Engineering or Astrophysics? Art Appreciation or Music Appreciation? So many young students think, "Whatever, it's an elective." When you've seen some of the world these choices become akin to seeing new menu items at your favorite restaurant. And the excitement you'll have when you first walk into a class that interests you is real and spectacular.

Cons:

- This is a tough one. The only noticeable con I see is that you'll be a few years older.

So as you can see, there are a lot of ways to get where you want to go. And in my opinion the only right answer is the one you choose for yourself.

False Starts – We Are Humans Being

Public celebrity or persona for athletes, entertainers, and even tech giants, focuses on their big smiling faces and awesome champagne and caviar lives. Only later, if ever, do we hear their journeys haven't been easy. And the journey I took to an awesome, happy life was no different. My trek from high school student to professional software engineer was not a straight-line path by any means. In the spring of my senior year of high school I applied and was accepted to a military junior college, Marion Military Institute. Nestled in a beautiful, southern town this then all-male college offered a two-year associate degree and U.S. Army Reserve Officer commissioning program.

Prior to attending, students completed Army Officer Basic training at Fort Knox, Kentucky. This is boot camp for officers. Cadets learn a lot about being a soldier and become very physically fit. When I attended we learned close order drill (marching and movements with rifles), land navigation, basic first aid, trained with the M16 rifle, M203 grenade launcher, M60 machine gun, hand grenades, the M72 LAW light anti-armor weapon, and M47 Dragon anti-tank weapon, learned night time escape and evasion, how to correctly bivouac or camp outdoors, basic survival skills, and more than anything else the importance of teamwork.

My drill sergeants were tough, experienced men who challenged us to our mental and physical limits daily. Several times we survived the hiking of two infamous hills; one named "Agony" and one named "Misery." Everything we did, we did as a team. And at the end of it I was in the best shape of my life.

In the fall I entered college as a freshman. Military school is exactly what you think it is- ninety percent of your day is planned and organized. It's a very efficient operation; reveille, breakfast, morning formation, classes, dinner (what we Yankees call lunch), more classes, afternoon formation, sports or other club activities, and supper followed by mandatory study and quiet time. If you are mentally focused on accomplishing your goals, this is a great environment. However, I wasn't. And being a young, eighteen year old Yankee in a comparatively competitive Southern environment, the lack of a buddy system for encouragement or accountability left some of us feeling isolated.

The first semester I earned A's, B's, and a C, a spot on their well-known White Knights drill team, and generally fit into the campus' lower socioeconomic echelon. I had enough money to attend the school but just $100 a month for discretionary things like clothing, shoes, toothpaste, and going out. *In hindsight, if I had been more focused on the purpose of my being there- to earn a great education- the lack of fun money would have been irrelevant.* Marion, Alabama is a really small town and on weekends there appeared to be little to do there. Each Friday night the more well off students sped off in their cars and didn't return till Sunday. The ones stuck on campus would watch HBO and MTV in the dorm, play video games in the campus snack shop, get a pick-up football game going, or stand guard duty at the gate. After a while I was completely bored out of my mind.

If I had been a little older I might have appreciated the wisdom of MASH TV's Colonel Sherman Potter, when he said, "If you ain't where you are, you're no place." So how does Colonel Potter's wisdom apply? Had I put in writing a set of goals with weekly milestones prior to starting school, that year could have gone quite differently. Simple goals such as earning a spot on the academic Dean's List, exploring college study-major options, writing my family more, and perhaps doing some volunteer work in town would have helped me keep focus. I didn't set goals or do any of those things and my second semester went poorly. Meeting with a representative in the Dean of Academics office I was offered two choices, retake the classes that had grades below C or become an enlisted man in the United States Army

Reserves. The Army has some fine traditions, however, my great uncles served in the Navy through the battles in the South Pacific during World War II. And serving at sea was always a dream of mine.

A perfectly fair question a reader might ask is, "If you liked the Navy more, why didn't you go in that direction first?" There were a couple of reasons. First, outside of the Naval Academy I didn't realize there were other ways to become a Naval Officer. We didn't have the internet available for researching things. Second, I didn't have the money for college. The loan for the first year at Marion Military Institute was co-signed by my parents, their money was tight too, and future years of college weren't discussed. That first year at Marion was my one, parent-supported shot and I had squandered it.

The weekend after the Dean's Office meeting I decided to visit to the Naval Recruiting station in Mobile, Alabama. The recruiter informed me active duty would supersede the reserves obligation. This meant I could go into the Navy instead of Army. He then arranged for me to take the Armed Forces Vocational Aptitude Battery (ASVAB); a multiple-aptitude test that measures developed abilities and helps predict future academic and occupational success in the military. After taking the exam, I waited in his office for the results. In a short period of time I noticed him walking towards me with a big grin- I'd crushed it. He then walked me through a cool book with all the Navy's ratings or career paths and said I could choose anything I liked. Cryptography? Yes! Computers + intel stuff + Navy = awesome.

Although my year at Marion Military Institute was wasted academically, the experience provided me the wisdom to focus on the things I really wanted and to not give up. *The lesson here for you is that there will be times when you're completely alone- with just your thoughts of planning and chasing your future. And as humans we sometimes make mistakes. Just don't give up; keep moving.*

PART III: FINDING MY FUTURE

Set Course

"Twenty years from now, you will be more disappointed by the things you didn't do than those you did. So throw off the bowlines. Sail away from safe harbor. Catch the wind in your sails. Explore. Dream. Discover." — *Mark Twain, Great American Writer*

The one thing I didn't realize about military service until I was half way through mine was likely the most important aspect. In the early years of one's service almost everything he does is a new experience. Drill Instructors, Lead Petty Officer (LPO), and one's Chief may be tough- like a boss who always seems to be cranky. But there's a really good reason for it. Like good football, basketball, or other sports coaches, they want us to be really strong members of the team. They want us to show our commitment and passion, the true spirit and heart exhibited by those completely into what they're doing. Once we appreciate that, and start living each day of our service in that mindset, everything falls into place and our futures know no bounds.

Navy Boot Camp – What It Was Like For Me

The first part of Navy Boot Camp was called Induction. Sailors arrive, receive lectures on proper behavior, the Navy's anti-drug policy, and back then we signed a final set of papers acknowledging our commitment to the training we were about to receive and service to which we were legally binding ourselves. For me this happened in sunny Orlando, Florida.

Over the many early hours we were issued uniforms, boots, sneakers, bedding, and more. By the time this was done it was very late at night and we were marched to barracks to crash for a few hours.

The next morning we received the outstanding haircuts for which the military is famous and began our Navy training in earnest. Four of my eighty shipmates decided this just wasn't for them. And we gave them the nickname, *The Over The Wall Gang*. Wearing their Navy-issue blue dungarees, blue cotton shirts, black boots, and sporting baldy haircuts they decided to flee; jumping the base fence in the middle of the night. You can imagine how quickly they were caught trying to walk to the Orlando bus station looking like four escaped convicts. After a day or so that was sorted out, we all laughed, and they were right back with us.

In boot camp they teach the baseline of things every sailor needs to know. In no particular order: The Uniform Code of Military Justice (UCMJ), making bunks, folding clothes, shining shoes, learning general orders, how to march, salute, stand a fire watch, navy ship types, areas on ships, types of missions the navy carries out, navy classifications / ratings, fire-fighting, damage control, swimming, PT or physical training, proper use of a pistol and a shotgun, battle stations / general quarters and more. Everyone receives a dental checkup, eye exam, shots, and information about the navy financial savings plan.

As part of our training we experienced something called One Five Day; first week, fifth day. It was testing that was a little physical but mostly mental. Inside the barracks we were inspected- as were our bunks and lockers. We were given a series of orders in rapid succession designed to see how we kept up and whether or not anyone would crack under pressure. The service requires everyone obtain top physical condition. Through training, those gifted with size naturally slim down and those weighing too little actually gain a few pounds.

Our company had one super large guy we instantly nicknamed "Tiny" and one small guy we nicknamed "Popeye." One of the important rules we followed was "No food in the barracks." Midway through our One Five Day inspection Tiny was busted for having five Snickers bars hidden in his laundry bag. We had no idea how he got his hands on them. The reaction from our Drill Instructors was straight out of the movie Full Metal Jacket and hilarious. They put us all in the push-up position and left us there to watch. For about fifteen minutes Popeye stood directly in front of Tiny and ate all five candy bars. While eating each one Popeye would moan, "Mmmmmmm" and tell us how tasty it was and Tiny would yell, "I promise never to eat in the barracks again!" And he never did- as we kept a vigilant eye on him.

When I went into the Navy I weighed two hundred eighteen pounds and was in okay shape. When we finished boot camp I weighed one hundred eighty eight pounds and was in fantastic shape. I remember being bored one Sunday during our free time so I started a push up contest. When a group of six of us got to seventy-five pushups we just started laughing and couldn't stop. The funny thing is we sailors were so focused on the mission, training and learning the Navy way, that we almost didn't notice the weight falling off.

Boot camp also teaches sailors how to follow and how to lead. Leadership roles in the company were Squad Leader, Master At Arms, and the top position called Recruit Chief Petty Officer (RCPO or "Poo"). Having three years of Navy Junior Recruit Officer Training Corps (NJROTC) in high school paid off in a big way. NJROTC high school training enabled sailors to come into the Navy two ranks higher than general recruits; starting as a Seaman (E3).

The lower ranks are: Seaman Recruit (E1), Seaman Apprentice (E2), and Seaman (E3). Petty officer ranks are above those. And then the officer ranks above those.

NJROTC training taught me all Navy ship and aircraft types, ranks and ratings, a sailor's general orders, formations, close order drill (marching), rifle positions, basic seamanship, and more. Having gone all-in in high school, these were things I knew forwards and backwards. One guy volunteered to be RCPO and that lasted about four hours. He gave it his best. Then I volunteered, earned it, and never looked back. Our company drilled better than any other I remember seeing and earned nearly every Recruit Company award available during boot camp. Little bits of success in each of the training phases served as the foundation of confidence. Our Drill Instructors built us up into an unstoppable part of the big Navy team. That confidence helps sailors during service and throughout their lives and I'm very grateful to them for the role they expertly played in training Orlando Company C235; August through November, 1982.

If you would like a more detailed description of the cool training provided at Navy Boot Camp, I invite you to visit the website *NavyForMoms.com*.

Cryptology: I Could Tell You But I'd Have To Shoot You

After boot camp sailors often go to their "A" school, the place they receive initial training in their rating or job. The Navy area I selected was cryptology. In the service this involves the collection, storage, and secure communication of intelligence information. We were and are called Cryptologic Technicians or CTs and in the fleet we are fondly referred to as "Spooks"; a common term for ghosts. There are different specific ratings within cryptology. Some sailors intercept various types of signals, some are linguists, some operate satellite and other equipment to disseminate information, and some maintain the equipment. At the time my rating was called CTO; cryptologic technician operator. We operated the equipment and communicated information twenty four hours a day, seven days a week.

In order to be able to operate computer equipment, the obvious skill one needs is typing. If you are interested in this line of work or anything to do with computers, it is worth the investment to build up your typing skills. You need the ability to quickly transition the ideas in your mind to your computer. Opportunities present themselves to the most productive engineers. *That's why keyboarding skills are so important.*

The first part of Crypto "A" School was, as you might guess, typing. This was taught in levels; up to thirty-five words per minute and then sixty. Within three or four weeks in I had improved to twenty-eight words per minute. I had tried and tried and but was just stuck at that level. My instructor called me into a meeting with three Chief Petty Officers interested in motivating me. Paraphrasing, the speech went a little like, "Sailor, if you don't type out in three days you'll find yourself as a Deck Ape on an Oiler so fast you'll be a distant memory in your family's minds." It worked. Two hours later I typed out at thirty-five words per minute. After that type out, we started formal "A" school classes and continued typing. Over the coming months I eventually finished at seventy-two words per minute.

The remainder of "A" school is a matter of protracted discussion. It's neat, job specific, and likely classified so we'll just move along. To demonstrate though an example of how hard work pays off, the Navy has a system to reward top academic performers. If a sailor was in the top ten percent of his class, he was invited to attend Crypto "C" school for advanced training. Motivated to make the most out of the Navy opportunity, I put in the extra time to earn this privilege. And it was well worth it.

Crypto "C" school was mostly for sailors from the fleet; first, second, and third class petty officers who had served at sea. These guys were an amazing addition to the learning environment because they gave us great insights into what we could expect- everything from the real-world cat and mouse games against the Russian Navy, to day-to-day shipboard life, to the best methods for aligning yourself when on temporary duty to the group with the more flexible liberty policy. *Note: While at sea we oftentimes weren't part of the permanent ship's compliment. We were either attached to an Admiral or General's staff or the ship temporarily. Working hard and playing hard, we CTs enjoyed trying to align ourselves with the group that maximized our free time; especially in foreign ports where we could enjoy liberty.*

"C" school taught us both tactical and strategic activities in which CTs participate along with how to use the latest and greatest computers, electronic equipment, and apps tailored to our mission. At the end of it, sailors went on to new assignments. Again, top academically-performing sailors earned first choice. This was the real deal- assignment to the fleet, perhaps an embassy, and there were many terrific choices; Hawaii, Spain, Italy, other countries and locations I cannot mention, as well as San Diego, California, Key West, Florida, and Norfolk, Virginia.

My choice was NSGD, CINCLANTFLT, Norfolk, Virginia or in layman's terms, Naval Security Group Detachment, Commander In Chief Atlantic Fleet, Norfolk, Virginia. CINCLANTFLT Norfolk was the heart and soul of the Navy on the East coast of the United States. The Tidewater Virginia area hosted dozens of bases and hundreds of commands- Army, Navy, Air Force, Marines, Coast Guard; all of them. The billet or specific position I choose was called "Direct Support." CTs in this position provide secure communications to Navy Admirals and Marine Corps Generals and sometimes are selected for other special missions. It's an awesome responsibility and opportunity. In the engineering world, you can think of Direct Support CTs as analyst-consultants. People with very specialized skills brought in for very specific tasks.

When on shore, we were assigned to a watch section. Shore watch sections provided similar services, just on land in a communications center. Watch sections worked an unusual set of shifts we called, two-two-two and eighty. That is two eight-hour day shifts, two eight-hour mid shifts, two eight hour eve shifts, followed by eighty hours off. It doesn't seem unusual until you mix in the fact there were only eight hours off between the day and first mid shift and only eight hours off between the second mid sift and the first eve shift. The eighty hours off time at the end was very nice and allowed us to do more interesting things such as three-day getaways or mini-vacations.

The Direct Support billet or position meant we also were assigned sea duty in a TAD or temporary additional duty status. From time to time opportunities to go to sea would present themselves. For us these were limited time, short term missions with another command. That having been written, there were assignments for CTs to be permanently assigned to some larger ships as well. NSGD Norfolk just had a different purpose and mission. While at sea we worked twelve hours on, twelve hours off, seven days a week.

Of course there are pros and cons to everything. On the one hand, those were a lot of hours but no more than the other sailors aboard worked. Some of the upsides to this kind of shift were we got to get a solid eight hours of sleep and since only the Captain and the Intelligence Officer had a security clearance high enough to enter our spaces, it was generally quiet enough for us to keenly focus on our intel-related activities. For some sailors, "quiet" actually means boring as hell. For others this represents opportunity. Think about it, how many aspiring sailors would have the chance to pick the brain of the commanding officer of a nuclear guided missile cruiser or a gigantic and complex marine amphibious assault ship? So when they came in, I surely did. The schedule of each commanding officer I met varied yet each one would come by for a briefing and stick around for a little bit. What better example to be around than someone who has worked super-hard to be in command of a billion dollar ship and hundreds or thousands of sailors?

Generally, relating this directly to you, that's what you want to do throughout the pursuit of your vision of the American Dream- put yourself around hard working people- those who have overcome obstacles and are always moving forward. Gravitate towards them. You can learn so much from them and they will inspire you.

Volunteering Vs. Being Assigned – Always Volunteer

If you want to be thought of as a stand-up, stand-out person then volunteer to take on challenging tasks- the kinds that cause others to sink low in their seats. Now I'm not writing about jumping up to get your Chief a cup of coffee and a doughnut. Any nimrod could do that. I mean tasks that make a difference and directly support the mission.

While on shore duty, a hidden away spot way back in our secure spaces had a large white board grid of upcoming missions. The board didn't provide specifics of the mission or where it might sail; just the ship name, approximate date of departure, and approximate length of assignment. Many of my shipmates would look at the board and turn away. Some wouldn't look it at all. *But I loved it!*

Why? Well let's think about this. When one hides from his duty only bad things happen. First, he earns a reputation as a slacker; someone who doesn't really care about the mission. Second, he usually gets stuck being assigned the worst of the worst duties. Sure, initially and especially in the lower ranks some of those more difficult assignments will come your way. There's no getting around that. Early on, I scrubbed a few heads (Navy bathrooms) and painted my fair share of curbs with yellow or white paint. These shared responsibilities rotate through the entire team and somedays it's just your turn.

However, volunteering earns you an opposite, good reputation as well. I used to look at that board all the time and say to my Chief, "Oh cool, a nuclear guided missile cruiser? I've never been on one of those. Gotta try that." Or "A marine amphibious assault ship leaving in October? Those are huge- almost the size of an aircraft carrier! I bet I could guess where they're headed." And what do you think happened when I started employing this outlook? You guessed it- my Chief started giving me MY choice.

The assignments were fantastic: Puerto Rico and the Panama Canal in the late summer, Spain in the fall, Sicily in the late spring, and the Arctic Circle and Norway in late January. Now I know some readers just shivered at the prospect of Norway in January. However, until you've seen Norway's deep black waters, tall and narrow fjords that have formed over several ice ages, and watched United States Marines conducting practice landings on their rocky shores in eight degree weather- you ain't seen nothin. A level of warmth consumed me one of those particular days as I peered through the port hole watching; hot chocolate in one hand and a bear claw pastry in the other. Those Marines are some tough dudes.

Volunteering helped my unit plan for missions and it helped me personally plan time off. Because the NSGD Norfolk Direct Support billet was state-side duty it counted as what the Navy considered a sailor's "preferred state-side shore tour." After a preferred state-side tour one was pretty much guaranteed his next tour would be at sea, overseas, or both. Given the amount of deployed sea time a Direct Support sailor accrued in this position, our unit had an informal policy of granting what we called *basket leave* or unofficial time off- one day per week a deployment lasted. There we're several times I deployed and came back with a couple weeks free vacation. This was pretty cool since it allowed me to bank my *regular leave* or vacation time.

Volunteering wasn't a completely selfless act. There was more than one occasion I volunteered for an October deployment to be home in time for Christmas or a May deployment to be home in time for a big family event in August. These were win-win scenarios for sure. In life you can't always control the *what* of what you are doing but you can oftentimes influence the *how*.

They Only Mess With You If They Like You

In the world of romance, one truism is that *hate is not the opposite of love, indifference is.* A similar truism with respect to friendship is that *people only mess with you if they like you.* Consider it in your daily life. Your real buddies bust on you, play jokes on you, give you outrageous nicknames, and more. People who are too busy, don't know you, or don't like you are ambivalent- they seem as though they couldn't care less. The same is true in day to day military life and this is just part of the fun.

The military provides ample opportunities to build *esprit de corps*, the feeling of pride and being part of a team, through sports, in one's daily job, and formal and informal parties. On our bases there were leagues for football, softball, basketball, volleyball, bowling, and more. And we regularly had company picnics and watch section parties. Sometimes these were for service members only and many times they were family-oriented affairs.

As for competition, there was definitely a pecking order and it went like this: country, service, command, rating. Inter-service rivalries were a big deal. My "A" and "C" school base had Army, Navy, Air Force, and Marine training groups and we regularly competed against each other; always talking trash. Trash talking was always part of the deal. On the CINCLANTFLT Headquarters base we were almost all Navy. So our commands would compete against each other. Cryptologists (spooks) vs submariners (bubble heads) vs Airmen (airdales) vs engineers (snipes); like that. The winners of our base sporting leagues would play in tournaments against the winners of other local bases. For example, my unit won the flag football championship for CINCLANTFLT Headquarters in 1985. And on that team I was the quarterback and the kicker.

Winning the base championship meant we got to go on to the regional tournament. In our first game we defeated another Navy unit. Our second game we beat an Air Force unit. And in our third game, although I kicked four field goals, we lost to the Navy Base Norfolk Marine unit that ended up winning the entire thing. The Marines were a good team and the score was a somewhat respectable 28-12. These events also represented opportunities to reinforce good sportsmanship. It was always the practice after every competition to say, "Good game," shake hands, and to offer your opponent good luck going forward. It was in those moments, at the end, we reaffirmed our membership as part of the bigger USA team and win or lose we always walked away feeling good.

Another benefit of the messing-with-you aspect was it helped us keep our edge and level of toughness. *When one is focused on a few important things such as his mission and his friends, his mind doesn't have a lot of time to wander.* And so it was within every command within which I served.

From 1983 to 1986 my unit included a few people who worked the day shift consistently and there were several rotating shift watch sections. Back then, our watch sections had about eighteen sailors each and at any given time a few from each section were deployed TAD on ships. Our two-two-two-and-eighty rotation meant we had four shifts.

The Chief of my watch section was CTOC James Vohland- outdoorsman, avid radio enthusiast, and mayor of Peppertown, Indiana. With extensive overseas duty (Kamiseya, Japan / Adak, Alaska / Keflavik, Iceland / Norfolk, Virginia) Chief Vohland was exactly the kind of leader, mentor, and Navy man every sailor hoped to meet. A consummate professional, he knew the Navy way for every part of our mission and had the right set of people skills; understanding just how to get the most out of our team in any given situation.

Every new sailor, me included, experienced a little initiation time. My Lead Petty Officer (LPO) CTO1 Chuck Casad, the senior sailor in our watch section ranking just below Chief Vohland, got me good. There are many ways the saltiness of a sailor, especially a shift working sailor, can be measured. Shift working sailors drink a lot of coffee to stay awake all night and virtually all of us had cool coffee cups- usually from a command or ship on which we served. Over time coffee stains or crud will build up, and I mean really build up, on the inside of the cup. The more crud there was, the more time he'd served, and the more salty a sailor he was. It was naval saltiness exemplified.

On my first shift, my LPO said the best way for me to get in good with my Chief was to make sure his cup got cleaned. So off I went to make a fresh pot of coffee- a task new sailors get as one of their first collateral duties. When I was done our LPO told the Chief a fresh pot had just been made and he went to get some. About thirty seconds later we all heard, "Son of a %$#^, what soon-to-be-dead #$#$%#& sailor scrubbed my cup!?" One doesn't get to be a Navy Chief without being able to determine what's what and he quickly surmised the LPO put me up to it. So we all had a good laugh and I was specifically instructed to stay the hell away from the Chief's cup. And I did.

Having been gotten good, I felt safe. That was my second mistake. Our LPO wasn't quite done breaking me in. One of our areas required us to maintain watch over incoming teletype traffic. For those unfamiliar, think of a teletype as an electronic typewriter (printer) that received decrypted signals and turned them into text. Our duties were to make sure the ink ribbons were in good shape, paper loaded, and most importantly to watch for high value message traffic requiring attention. My LPO told me there was rumor of Russian aircraft activity and I should keep a keen eye out for messages about their B1RDs and GU11s. For the next two hours, in John Paul Jonesian style I ardently manned my post- refusing to take a break so that we could help pinpoint these commie rascals. And about every half hour my LPO would come by to check in and offer encouragement although on the other side of the equipment rack I started hearing some good laughing. What a fun bunch I thought- we work hard, we play hard.

And then it dawned on me. Oh no, they wouldn't. Yes, B1RDs are "birds" and GU11s are "gulls." He got me again. Twice in one day. Okay, now I knew how they rolled. But you know what? Petty Officer First Class and eventually Chief Casad was always there to teach us as well. So the saying is true, they only mess with you if they like you.

My First Mission Was The Hardest

What I'm about to describe is the most difficult thing I've experienced in my life. But you need to read this- all of it.

From the summer of 1983 to the same time in 1984 I was engaged to be married to my girlfriend from high school. In June of 1984 I had been with NSGD Norfolk, at CINCLANTFLT Headquarters for a bit but had not yet deployed. The command was accommodating in letting me take leave or vacation to get married in my home area of Cape May County, New Jersey. We were to then enjoy a little time afterwards for a honeymoon in sunny, yet affordable, Norfolk, Virginia.

The weekend started off fantastically. My parents hosted a small rehearsal dinner at the home of an aunt and uncle and we had an amazing turnout of family and well-wishers. Afterwards all of us in the wedding party went to the boardwalk in Wildwood to have some fun. That night I learned my youngest sister, Wendy, was so impressed with my Navy experience she was going to sign up herself. Pretty darn cool, huh? The wedding and reception went well and the morning after we followed the tradition of opening gifts and making note of each sender so we could write very nice thank you cards. Then later that afternoon we packed up everything we could and headed on down to Norfolk. That was Sunday.

Tuesday, two days later, we were in middle of setting up our first apartment when there was a knock at the door. It was my commanding officer and my LPO. They came to let me know some very bad news. My mom and sister were on their way to the Navy recruiting station in Atlantic City when they were hit head-on by three drunk kids from Philadelphia.

My mom died at the scene and my sister, Wendy, was in the hospital for months. Two of the three drunk kids died instantly and the third died two days later. We utilized my remaining leave time to travel to where my family had moved in South Alabama for my mother's funeral. On the way back our car died out in the middle of no-where Western Virginia. It took almost every penny of the $850 we had to get the car fixed and we had to take a bus back to Norfolk.

I was a mess and so was the start to our marriage all due to three drunk kids headed down to the shore. They ruined that part of our lives, killed themselves, and ruined the lives of their own families– all for some beer. Idiots.

We struggled for a few days as I zombied my way through work shifts. No one quite knew what to say to me and I think Chief Vohland realized morale was starting to tail spin. Like a horse healing from a broken leg, I was either going to run again or I wasn't and they needed to know. So two weeks later they deployed me as part of a crypto team to the USS Glover FF-1098.

At first I felt abandoned. Then I felt I was abandoning my new bride in a new town with no friends and no money. And then I felt ticked off. *In hind sight it was the best thing the Navy could have done.* My wife went back to visit with her mom for a while and I carried on with the mission.

Meeting the USS Glover proved to be an interesting trip in itself. We flew to San Juan, Puerto Rico wearing civilian clothes, on a commercial airliner. From there we hired a local, unregulated, full-service taxi driver to take us to the Navy base a couple hours away. When I write, "unregulated," I mean the cab had no hub caps and the driver popped open the trunk where he had a case of adult beverages on ice for us ready to enjoy during the ride. Mr. Not-Drinking Taxi Driver drove 90 mph almost the entire way and there were a few times we weren't sure we were going to make it around tight bends and without hitting oncoming traffic or local farm animals.

On arrival at Roosevelt Roads Navy Base we checked in, got our rooms in the barracks, and wondered what to do next. The ship wasn't in and we were then informed it was going to be three days late. Puerto Rico in August is hot- not Texas hot but Jurasic Park jungle hot with birds and all kinds of cool wildlife. Having missed dinner the first night, we asked some of the Navy base personnel where we might go to get something to eat. They mentioned a dive bar-restaurant about a mile up the road so off we went on foot. One of the fantastic benefits of being in the Navy is the chance to see the world. Until now, Puerto Rico was only a tropical vacation destination I'd read about in brochures and I must say the advertising one sees doesn't do the country justice. When you get out into the rural areas, it's a beautiful place.

The restaurant we found was a family-owned, local hole in the wall kind of place and looked like it would have had a tough time withstanding the next good Caribbean breeze to hit the island. But there was no mistaking this was a good place to eat. The scent of classic Puerto Rican cuisine filled the air and as none of us spoke Spanish, we politely asked our waitress to help us choose something. Within minutes, she brought sopón de pollo con arroz, a chicken soup with rice that was simply amazing. It was one of those soups one enjoys slowly; savoring every spoonful. If you have tasted something like this you know exactly what I mean. The soup was followed by beef-filled empanadillas. These are crescent shaped turnovers and were equally good. As it was getting dark and there were few street lights between the restaurant and the base, we thanked our waiter, tipped her very well, and made our way back to the base.

By the time we got back, night had fallen. Only a single lightbulb lit the outside concrete porch area, however, there was something new- a large trashcan filled with ice and beer right outside our door. A gift perhaps? They had one heck of a Navy base welcoming committee. We drug the can into our room and began to relax. One of my shipmates fumbled around looking for the light switch as I made my way to one of the bunk beds in the dark.

It had been a long day of travelling and getting situated and I just wanted to crash. One of my fellow CTs said, "The room looks funny, like it's moving." Ignoring him I flopped on the bottom bunk and instantly what seemed like twenty, six-inch-long, walking stick bugs rained down on me and started crawling everywhere. We all freaked, running out of the room. After a minute we found the light switch, turned it on, and saw what looked to be hundreds of them; on the bunks, on the walls, on our gear, absolutely everywhere. Thankfully, the light made them scatter. Walking stick bugs are indigenous to Puerto Rico and are nocturnal creatures. They are generally still during the day and forage for food at night. That night, the light stayed on and we enjoyed the free beer provided by the welcoming committee.

Early the next morning, we learned the beer wasn't really free. We awoke to find four highly-torqued off United States Marines in the adjoining room. They were on temporary duty (TAD) as well and very interested in determining what became of their beer. Thankfully, before things got interesting, a Petty Officer from the base arrived and we were unceremoniously sucked into a work detail; mowing lawns on the Navy Base for the entire day. When we came back, the Marines were nowhere to be found. Wiped out from what regular sailors might call "real work" we crashed hard.

With the dawn of the next day the USS Glover had pulled into port and we checked in- as did those same Marines. Having only met Infantry Marines this was quite a shock to me. These were highly-trained Spanish linguists- smart *and* capable of kicking 100% of our collective asses. This was going to be an interesting mission.

Leaving Purto Rico we set sail for a small port town in the country of Honduras. The Navy pays it forward in lots of ways most people never hear about. In this case a very small, very poor seaside town needed some help. When I write poor, I mean third-world poor- not America's I've got a flat screen but I can't afford HBO and Cinemax poor. Most of the buildings and homes were of wood and worn cinderblock construction, had dirt or rotten wood floors, limited running water, few real windows, and electricity generally consisting of a single-lightbulb-terminated wire dangling down from the ceiling. Our mission was to build a school for them. Aboard the USS Glover we carried everything necessary; lumber, concrete, electrical wiring, you name it. We did our level best for three days with lots of sailors happily pitching in. It's one of the coolest things we did almost no one heard about; till now.

Heading South and East, we made our way towards the Panama Canal. The USS Glover was a Garcia class frigate, originally modified just for research use and commissioned on November 3, 1965. Fitted with advanced sonar and other gear, she was a platform designed to test new anti-submarine weapons systems and explore their tactical uses for future fleet use. Over the years she experienced several updates and in 1979 became the then FF-1098. The Captain wanted to make sure everything was good to go for our mission so for a week straight we held multiple general quarters drills every day and conducted lots of weapons testing. And we're glad he did. The single 5" gun had issues. It would be fired two times and then be down for a day and a half. The Phalanx CIWS (close in weapons system), a Gatling-style gun capable gun capable of firing thousands of rounds per minute, kept jamming and repeatedly had to be taken apart. But the Gunners Mates of the Glover were on it and eventually got things ship shape.

As we were headed to the Pacific Ocean, we traversed through the Panama Canal. Just FYI, traversing the Panama Canal is definitely worth trying on a luxury cruise or Navy ship sometime. On each side of the Panama Canal is lush jungle, teaming with wildlife; capuchin and spider monkeys, colorful macaws and parrots, brown pelicans, crocodiles, and lots and lots of water snakes. The weather there is perfect for them and if you like it hot, this is the place to be. During the day, mind you this was mid-August, it was ninety-nine degrees with one hundred percent humidity. In the evening it cooled off to a balmy ninety-two. The trip takes several days, depending upon shipping traffic, and watching the locks fill to raise or lower your ship accordingly is a pretty interesting thing.

Once on the Pacific Ocean side of the Panama Canal, we were told our true mission. From roughly 1979 and into the 1990's, the anti-Communist Nicaraguan Contras fought against the pro-Communist Sandinista National Liberation Front. This was 1983. Many experts in the United States and the world for that matter saw this as a potential tipping point in Central America. The Russians, from the other side of the world, had begun providing the Sandinistas with MI-24 attack helicopters (Hinds), Mi-17 transport helicopters, supplies, training, and more.   They were threatening their neighbor to the North, El Salvador. Many Americans and others feared the domino theory- that one country falling to the communists would lead to another and another and this would become a reality that would threaten freedom and spread equality of misery throughout the region. As part of the tip of the spear protecting freedom, we weren't going to let it happen.

To this day there is much political disagreement around the ends justifying tactical means employed by some of the Contras to fight the Communists. War is never pretty and this one was much like every other with atrocities on both sides. It is a matter of public record that the United States worked hard to unite the disparate Contra groups into a more functional force and in the end, due to this is and other factors outside the region, the Nicaraguan threat to El Salvador waned. This is my view as someone who was there for just a few months. For a more complete perspective I invite you to read about this history online at the Encyclopedia Britannica website.

The mission was the mission and we did our best, working twelve hours a day, seven days a week, in ninety-plus degree heat. We were sweaty in the daytime, sweaty in the night time- and stinky all the time. Although working the night shift, I wasn't excused from our continuous, unannounced, daytime general quarters (GQ) drills. These happened so often we nightshift guys began to sleep in uniform. For Cryptologists, our GQ station was our duty station so when the alarm sounded we jumped out of our racks, stepped into our boondocker shoes, and scrambled to our battle stations. Oftentimes twice a day for a couple of hours we sat half-asleep in the high heat, wearing gas masks, with our dungaree pants tucked into our socks and shirts buttoned up in an attempt to limit injury from a potential chemical attack. After a while we began to joke this was better than any weight loss program a gym might offer. And the Navy provided it *free.*

Appreciating how extended time on station could wear a crew down, the Navy had a cool rule to help. Back then if a ship were underway more than ninety days, each crewman was offered two beers. Normally alcohol wasn't permitted on a Navy ship at all. Day ninety-two was really fun one. That Sunday, the Captain approved something Navy guys call a Steel Beach Picnic. It's a cook out topside, where the ship's metal deck is the beach, and these events usually included lots of interesting activities.

My night shift ended early Sunday morning and I headed for the mess decks for breakfast. Breakfast was my absolute favorite meal of the day because the Navy did a really good job with it. Eggs were available almost any way you liked them as were waffles, pancakes or French toast, fruit, and bacon and sausage. And it was all really good stuff. After breakfast, I always went topside to watch the Sun come up and enjoy a little fresh air. But Steel Beach Picnic day was different.

As I climbed the long, grey ladder to the deck with our helicopter hangar, I caught the unmistakable scent of something special- slowly roasting pork barbecue ribs. One of the ship's Chiefs, a particularly large and strong man, was babysitting racks and racks of ribs the way a T-Rex mother might guard her young. No one was getting anywhere near those ribs till the Chief decided it was time. I approached cautiously and from an angle, offering compliments on how they looked, and asked him how it was going. Proudly he told me it was a complex, involved process deserving one's full attention. I then made the mistake of asking him the secret of his rub. With a big laugh and a slight "na-na-na" finger wave he invited me to leave. I didn't blame him at all for that- my mouth was already watering. A meal on the mess decks can make or break a sailor's tough day, however, slow roasted ribs with just the right rub, char, and sauce are a very rare treat. So I obeyed the Rib Master in hopes of sampling what he'd later deliver.

The Glover's Steel Beach Picnic was a lot of fun in a surreal kind of way. The latest music was cranking on a sound system, there was swimming off the fantail or back of the ship, guys were catching some sun and playing cards, and a few guys were deployed on the upper decks with rifles in case sharks showed up. For a while the Captain was even letting us water ski behind his personal barge. The ship had another barge too- one much larger that was for general use. Since alcohol wasn't to be consumed on board, guys were taking turns climbing down a rope ladder into the larger barge to enjoy their two beers.

Perhaps it was the beer or the ninety-two straight days at sea but at some point someone decided it would be a good idea to hold a fishing contest on the bow of the ship. And to increase the chances catching some really good ones, chum was being dumped into the water. Now it doesn't take a math genius here to figure the odds of things going awry when there's less than 400 feet between a fishing contest and a bunch of sailors flopping around in the water.

In confused disbelief I just shook my head, traded my two beers for another big portion of those succulent ribs, and sat back to watch the show. Turns out they did use someone with math skills better than mine, somehow there were no sharks, and the Steel Beach Picnic was a big hit with the entire crew.

After we completed the remainder of our mission, we sailed North to Acapulco, Mexico for a liberty call. As we were getting close to port, we CTs negotiated amongst ourselves how we'd work our liberty time. There was a two-man rule for our gear, supplies, and data. There had to be two men in our Crypto spaces at all times. Other than that there wasn't much activity going on. One of our Marine friends commented for about the twentieth annoying time how he wished he knew what became of their Puerto Rican beer investment and it was all I could take. At that point we had become good friends so I called him a "wuss" and said we'd take them out drinking if he'd just stop whining about it. And then I confessed to our taking their beer. For a few seconds they sat quietly, looking at each other. Then they laughed too- agreeing to the night-of-free-beer deal. Whew!

Wow, just wow. The Acapulco beaches, local hospitality, and Mexican culture all made for an outstanding experience. We explored the city, met a lot of locals, and enjoyed some wonderful, authentic Mexican cuisine. Later that afternoon we learned it was Bull Fight day and we went to the stadium to check it out.

There was a lot of color, pomp, and ceremony to it. The venue seemed about the size of an American football stadium and various refreshments were available including some agave-flavored water called Mezcal which, oddly, had a worm in the bottom of the bottle.

There a bullfight is called a "Corrida." Six bulls are fought by three matadors. And the matadors have five assistants; three banderilleros and two picadors. Each fight starts with a trumpet blast to begin the parade of the bullfighters. The second trumpet blast precedes the entrance of the bull. The chief assistant is the first person to approach the bull and he tests the bull's mood, speed, power and agility. During this, the matador is watching very carefully to see how the bull reacts.

The third trumpet signals the arrival of picadors, men on horseback who carry steel-tipped, long pikes. Their job is to weaken the muscle between the shoulder blades of the bull so his head hangs low; making him less of a threat. To put this in NBA basketball terms it's the equivalent of the ball boy coming out at warm ups and kicking LeBron James in the shin while wearing steel-tipped boots just to see what kind of mood he's in. *Not cool.*

Bullfights are the real deal- there's real blood, real carnage, and eventually real death. The first one I saw almost made me gasp. Midway through the second one, being human, I felt angry and helpless to do anything about it. By the third one I was ticked off. Two-thirds of the way through our large bottle of agave water, my friends and I witnessed something extraordinary. To start the fourth battle, it looked as though a picador was brought out of retirement. The guy looked like he was ninety years old if he was a day. And the bull was a pretty strong one. Sensing a bit of fair play we moved to the edge of our seats.

Grandpa picador, as we called him, approached, circled, and made his move to strike first. He did, and the bull became royally torqued-off. The picador poked again. And then it happened! The bull charged full force, catching his horse straight on, nearly throwing grandpa to the ground. We jumped to our feet and yelled, "Woot! Woot! Woot!"

It was at that moment we realized we didn't know everything about Mexican culture. A dozen or so local men sitting behind us told us in no uncertain terms it was poor form to root for the bull and not to do it again. To paraphrase American comedian, Ron White, we couldn't tell how many of them it would take to kick our butts but we could tell how many they were planning to use. So we chilled out.

The one upside worth noting about bullfights was after each round the restaurant to which the bull was being taken was announced. In America, competitions are best when they are somewhat evenly matched and if they aren't one should cheer for the underdog because the superior team or person is expected to win. That's just good sportsmanship. There are a lot of things I respect and even revere about Mexican culture but bullfighting isn't one of them. Want most Americans to respect bullfighting? Make it mano e mano- one matador, one bull, no extras. Then we'll see where the machismo lives.

To be fair though and to digress a bit, over the past twenty years we Americans have embraced UFC fighting; humans practically killing other humans. Our cognitive abilities to advance reason seem to have really outpaced our body's other genetic evolution and in many ways Western societies have done a lot to emasculate men; compelling us to suppress virtually all emotion. UFC popularity could reasonably be considered the pendulum swinging back the other way. At least with Mexican bullfighting the result is a fine steak dinner, so let me raise of my agave water glass with a salute: ¡ viva méxico!

All this having been written, the end of our port call to Acapulco was the beginning of our trip home. We sailed from there southward, back through the Panama Canal, stopping off in Guantanamo, Cuba briefly to refuel. And then we headed back to Norfolk, Virginia. After coming home, there were plenty of nights I stepped outside of my apartment to look at the stars. I remembered the wife, mother, friend, 4-H Leader, nurse, and great person my mom was and I prayed for someone to wake me from this bad dream.

Lesson: When one drinks and drives it's not just his life he could ruin. Although I had lost arguably the most important person in my life I did gain something new- my Navy family. New, different, respectable, and good.

The Art Of The Deal

From 1962 to 1966, long before most of us were born, actors Ernest Borgnine, Joe Flynn, and Tim Conway helped create a very funny television show about the misadventures of a misfit Navy PT Boat crew during World War II. It was called McHale's Navy and tons of episodes can be found free to enjoy on YouTube. In the show, the crew of the PT-73 completed their missions, however, they were always looking for fun and trouble; usually in the form of gambling or chasing women. This usually resulted in them making crazy deals to get whatever they wanted. Now I'm not going to say which ships and which missions but in some cases my real life ship activity somewhat mimicked this television show.

By Tom Nicholas

As with many aspects of communications, the classified nature of equipment used preclude me detailing specific capabilities but even in the 1980's we Crypto guys had real time connectivity worldwide. This is no national secret. Basic information was as valuable an asset back then as it is today and there were two things sailors wanted to know; sports scores and real news from home. This kind of information was drizzled out ship-wide in a very limited, very controlled kind of way. And my best guess is the officers felt the need to manage emotional state of the crew- to keep us balanced and mentally focused. Hypothetically, it would be easy to fathom that learning the 1985 Buffalo Bills football team had gone 2-14 for a second consecutive year could have driven Petty Officer Third Class Mark Russell from Lackawanna to dive off the port quarter and go chew on an ice berg. Internalizing the risk, basically blowing it off, both the Chiefs and First Class Petty Officers wanted more depth of news and sports information anyway. And in true entrepreneurial spirt I provided this service through the "testing" of backup reception equipment including older short wave radio sets.

My personal preference was to work the night shift, usually 1800 hours to 0600 hours; six at night to six in the morning. It was less busy then and offered peace, quiet, and the opportunity to study my rating for advancement. After about 2200 hours almost no one came into our spaces till around 0500 hours. That's when the Captain would come in to review traffic; a kind of morning briefing.

The *mess area* on a Navy ship refers to the place where a particular group of sailors eat; *Enlisted mess, First Class Petty Officer's mess, and Chief's mess* respectively. For officers this place is called the *Wardroom.*

On one of my ships, the First Class mess was interested in sports scores. Like most every private sector company for which I've worked, they had betting pools where people picked winners of games and the person with the best overall selections won a pot of money. I could get the information to them more quickly than the Radiomen so I negotiated the data for an entire tray of fresh, sweet, cinnamon-almond bear claws. Each morning at 3 AM, we made the exchange- data for pastry. Similarly the Chief's mess wanted news from around the world and especially back home; the kind of reporting one might see on Fox News or CNN. In exchange for this, they offered me access to their library of over one thousand movies.

Coffee + bear claws + movies = awesome relaxation. That is, until the Commanding Officer decides to review his communications at 4 AM instead of 5 AM. One night I was in the last twenty minutes of the WWII Lee Marvin movie classic,

36

"The Dirty Dozen," feet up, bear claw in one hand, coffee in the other, when the Captain walked in. He said, "Nice, this is just about the end of the movie, huh." Dropping the bear claw and coffee and *jumping to attention* I responded, "Yes sir." Although all my work was caught up, the Captain still considered this activity a little over the line and suggested I end the practice. The Captain never again came in early- I knew that he knew that I knew that his suggestion was *more than just a suggestion.* Although movie nights abruptly ended I lived up to my offer with the Chiefs and First Class Petty Officers, maintaining our great relationship, and the bear claws remained as tasty as ever.

Lesson: Always look for opportunities to create win-win scenarios. Sometimes the deals won't go completely as planned, however, whenever possible stick to your side of the deal for the long term, greater good. And yes, as an actor Lee Marvin totally rocked.

Of Ladders And Universal Gyms And Things

Deploying to sea always brought with it a bunch of emotion. I'd think about the friends and family I was leaving behind, the experiences I'd miss with them, and about those I was about to have with my shipmates. We had a general idea of where we were heading but usually not specifics and it was all but impossible to imagine what might happen next. When would the Russian ships catch up and start tailing us? What world event might require our attention? In the movie, "The Hunt For Red October" there's a scene where the Russian Captain, played by Sean Connery, speaks to his crew, "Once more, we play our dangerous game, a game of chess against our old adversary — The American Navy." For me, deployments felt exactly like that- it was always a great mysterious challenge. The Russians would hunt for us and we'd hunt for them, always sizing each other up and looking for tactical weaknesses- knowing full well that if the situation required it and they so much as twitched the wrong way, our commanding officers would have blown them half way to Mars. And that kept us on-point, focused, and having fun.

What also kept it fun was messing with them. Rumor was, back then the Russians didn't get to visit as many exciting liberty ports as we did. So from time to time practical jokes just kind of happened. For example, we were supposed to put lots of holes in anything tossed overboard in the middle of the Atlantic so as to not disclose any classified information. The Russians would come in behind us and try to scoop whatever they could out of the water before it sunk to the bottom. Knowing they didn't get much in the way of mail we sometimes shared our unwanted Popular Mechanics and Sports Illustrated Swimsuit edition magazines, making sure to clip out parts that might tempt them to stray from their duties and jump overboard to swim to America. And in fine sailor tradition they would give the international, single-fingered, we're-number-one wave of thanks back to us.

I recall a few times though, hauling my fifty pound sea bag up a gangplank to report aboard a new command feeling I wasn't as fit as I was the day I left boot camp. When in port we worked rotating shift work which included weekends and overnight. Half the team were married with families and we only seemed to do physical training or PT *together* in the weeks leading up to our annual fitness test. So over time, the extra pounds start to add up. One of the good things about being temporarily assigned to other commands at sea was that while underway we got much more exercise and seemed to eat less often. Our temporarily-assigned berthing was usually a couple of decks below the waterline and our work spaces several decks above it in the ship's superstructure. Navigating between them meant climbing six to eight ladders or metal sets of steps. This was great exercise. Also, no matter what we needed or wanted, be it supplies or a simple can of soda, it seemed to be three decks down and twenty or thirty sections forward or aft. More good exercise. And in my free time I simply liked the endorphin release exercise brought.

Ships generally have some kind of gym and the larger the ship, the better the equipment. Generally I found the universal equipment much safer than using free weights. The restricted movement of that equipment meant it wasn't going to go flying when we hit some rough seas. The fun part though was timing your lifts with the movement of the ship. Pushing at the wrong time felt like you were lifting twice the weight and pushing at the right time felt like the weights were going to fly up in the air. This inevitably led to joking and busting on each other in colorful ways only sailors can about being weak or super strong and these small moments of levity kept up our morale.

The great upside to all of this is coming home from deployment I was always much more fit and a good ten to fifteen pounds lighter. Call it a *Navy perk*. Working through extended times away from home, with my shipmates, created a great bond which made us all better in lots of ways. *Reality can be the perception you create.* I chose to, as they say, always see the glass as half full. You can take that choice through the challenging times in your life too. There are always upsides if you choose to see them.

How To Impress The United States Marine Corps

Many of the missions on which I embarked were in support of Navy-Marine Corps joint deployments transiting the Atlantic and into the Mediterranean Sea. These included larger LPH (Landing Platform Helicopter) and LHA (Amphibious Assault) ships such as the USS Iwo Jima LPH 2, USS Guam LPH 9, USS Inchon LPH 12, USS Saipan LHA 2, USS Nassau LHA 4 which carried thousands of Marines, helicopters, and their other combat equipment.

As one could imagine, thousands of Marines and Navy sailors in the middle of the Atlantic for weeks on end, not fighting anyone, and without a liberty port in sight can eventually make for an antsy bunch. So events were whipped up to take our minds of that. One such idea was the "smoker"- a set of boxing matches between the Navy and Marines. The stereotype of the infantry Marine being the kind of guy who chews metal and spits barbed wire is pretty much dead on. So when it came to boxing, that's what we were going up against.

Equally stereotypical is the dedicated, red headed, Irish kid from Boston who's been boxing since the age of seven. And on one of our trips, as this true story goes, we had a really good one.

For this smoker, the equipment in the gym had all been pushed aside and a ring set up. Boxers used headgear, good gloves, and the rules were carefully spelled out. Bout after bout went to the Marines and most of them weren't even close until the Boston Kid. The matches were three rounds each. And every Marine fought exactly the same way; hard and fast with the intent of ending it as quickly as possible. The trick was to simply survive the first round. With skills reminiscent of Muhammad Ali, the Boston Kid floated like a butterfly, stung like a bee, and rope-a-doped through the Marine pummel technique. At the end of the first round the Marine was starting to wear down. All his buddies were telling him to just continue their tactic, that sooner or later he'd land a good punch.

From across the ring the Boston Kid only offered a blank stare- and not even a smile. "Ding!" went the bell for round two. And the Marine went at it again like a Tasmanian Devil. However half way through he started getting tired, sloppy, and began dropping his arms. Without missing a beat the Boston Kid started taking advantage of it. First a quick jab, then another, and then a wicked-awesome New England hook. By the end of the second round he was controlling the bout and describing the Marines as animated would be an understatement. Their unbeaten record was on the line as was their reputation. And to United States Marines, reputation means a lot. They've been building one for excellence since November 10th, 1775.

The Marines figured out they needed to box, really box, and they frantically gave true boxing advice to their comrade. But it was too late. This Marine fell into the Boston Kid's carefully laid trap. Round three started out evenly for about forty-five seconds and then the Boston Kid absolutely went off; pounding the Marine relentlessly. He didn't knock him out but by the end of the round there was no doubt who won the match.

The final bell rang and the Navy side went nuts with cheers, hoots, and hollers as if we'd just won the Super Bowl. And at the end of the event, the senior NCOs of both the Marines and Navy congratulated the combatants and we all shook hands. That day the Navy earned the respect of the Marine detachment onboard. For the next few months anytime the topic of sports would come up in the chow line someone would say, "You know, I hear boxing is making a come back..." and we'd get back the expected, "Yeah, yeah, yeah."

Lesson: Brains can beat brawn. Thoughtful, carefully executed plans, especially in the business world, will beat the bull in a china shop approach to most any problem.

How Not To Impress The United States Marine Corps

Terror, fright, panic, trepidation, dread, consternation, dismay, and distress- within a four minute period and through an act completely of my own doing I was able to infuriate a senior Marine Corps Gunnery Sergeant into filling my mind with all of these things and into making me think he was about to toss me overboard. The final leg of a Med Cruise (Mediterranean deployment) from Rota, Spain back to the United States represents an opportunity for units to make everything ship shape and Bristol fashion so most sailors and Marines can take leave time upon getting home. During this time, both equipment and personnel inspections are completed. However, even with the best of intentions, things don't always go as planned.

One sunny morning, just three days away from arriving home, I'd completed the night crypto shift aboard the USS Guadalcanal (LPH-7), the third of the large, Iwo Jima-class amphibious assault ships. The ship had announced a short period of time to dispose of waste and there were only a few minutes left so I moved as quickly as I could to haul away a forty pound bag of shredded paper.

Unbeknownst to me, a full Company of Marines and two of their CH-53 Sea Stallion helicopters were in final preparations on the hangar deck for their big inspection. The deck had just been hosed down, the helicopters glistened, and the Marines looked impressive.

As I quickly made my way by them I was told, "Move, move, hurry up- we have an inspection about to start!" Having reached the edge of the ship on the other side of the hangar bay, I began to tear holes in the big bag of paper shred. You can guess where this is going.

The ship rocked to port, then to starboard, then to port, and then back to starboard. Each time it did a big gust of wind would go one way, and then the other. Timing my toss carefully, I flung the bag with all my might off the port side. I then turned and took about three steps before a hurricane of shredded paper went whizzing by me immediately covering the deck, the Marines, and every wet nook, cranny, and crevice of their beautiful CH-53 Sea Stallion helicopters.

Within seconds I met their company's version of Full Metal Jacket's Gunnery Sergeant Hartman and I was about to play the role of Private Joker. I had screwed up and any response I could give would have been one hundred percent full of *"wrong answer."* He started yelling and I came to attention, just stood there, and took it. His righteous stream of impossible human contortionist instructions, some requiring my head be separated from the rest of my body, blew through me at ninety miles per hour. Eventually two Marines pulled him back. All I said was, "Gunny, I'm sorry."

He asked for my name and department. They sent two Marines up to my spaces to let my unit know I was going to be busy for a while. For the next eight hours I picked up thousands and thousands of pieces of shred. The error was all on me and I manned up and accepted it. Part way through the afternoon a squad of extra-duty guys, sailors who had gotten in trouble separately, joined in to help. At the end of the day the Gunny came back by to see how it was going and I apologized again. All we could do was laugh- well I did, long after he left.

On the mess decks and in my own unit I had become infamous- earning the thumbs up and several, "That's him, that's the guy!" But it was okay. I earned it, I took it, and I survived and learned from the experience. But I never made the same mistake again.

Lesson: Even with your best planning, sometimes things will go poorly. When they do you must step up and own your role in it. Don't duck any part of it and be sincere in your apology. Seek to learn and improve from the experience. This builds character, strengthens you for tougher challenges, and serves as an excellent example to others. Your integrity must be non-negotiable because it's the foundation upon which the best-you you can be is built.

Hurricanes, Saltines, And The Radiomen Rivalry

There are few things more foreboding and ominous to a sailor than navigating his ship through a thick fog. In the summer of 1985 I was selected for a mission aboard the USS Belknap CG-26 where we engaged in one of the most-cool war games I'd ever experienced. The Belknap and one other ship were fitted with cool new equipment and we were to go up against more than a dozen other ships. Our mission was simple: target the other ships without being targeted ourselves.

At the time, the crypto spaces onboard the Belknap were not permanently manned. Although there were racks welded to the deck, we had to bring most of our own equipment. And although there were a couple desks, there were no chairs. Moving quickly, we checked ourselves into the ship, got our equipment set up and checked out, and prepared to get underway. For chairs, our LPO visited the Radiomen who were happy to help; in a left-handed sort of way. With a bunch of them grinning, they gave us a nice set of chairs- all with wheels on them. Now we CTs prided ourselves on knowing things before other sailors did, but those smiles on the Radiomen made us begin to wonder- what didn't we know? While the ship was tied to the pier, chairs with wheels would be awesome, however, we'd all been in the North Atlantic before and knew we needed something more; rope. Gladly someone in the Deck Department was willing to give us some rope and we lashed the chairs to the equipment racks. Easy peasy, right? *Not so fast sports fans.*

There was a Navy Admiral on board and it was announced the reward for winning the exercise would be a port call in Halifax, Nova Scotia- the crown jewel of the island in the eastern part of Canada. We started out in the vicinity of Bermuda and the Command announced we were going to use a passing tropical storm to our tactical advantage- by literally hiding in it.

The Belknap was sharp. For the age of the ship I was amazed how well both she and her crew seemed to function as one. Everything was in its place and every man seemed to know exactly what he was doing. They were definitely all business; *Navy business.* Preparing to live in the tropical storm, we started battening down the hatches so to speak- boxing up and tying down anything and everything that might go flying. Our tactical exercise began and headlong into the teeth of the storm we sailed. The seas grew higher and higher and lightening, in intensity I'd never seen, began to forebodingly strike all around us. Once our storm preparations were completed, we headed down to the mess decks; six levels below our spaces.

That evening the better dinner option was thick, slow-roasted, pork chops in a devil may care gravy partly of its own renderings. The meat part was very good and thanks to its coating each morsel slithered down our throats with ease as the storm topside continued. Back in our duty spaces, with each swell the ship heaved to port, to starboard, up, down, and even sideways at times; as did our dinner. My LPO and one of the other senior petty officers in our detachment noticed some of us were starting to turn pale and eventually green. This felt like one of those spinning carnival rides that had no end. Not missing an opportunity to show us their interest, they started asking how much we enjoyed the pork chops- descriptively reminding us how they sloshed around in the heavy, browned grease. Now when a CT is on duty, he's on duty- there are no time-outs, no do-overs, and no I'll-catch-you-next-times.

Being tied to one of the wheeled chairs, itself lashed to the equipment rack, I had no quick escape. And then the unwanted happened- up I threw, gobs of pork chop and green beans on the keyboard, on the screen, on myself; everywhere. G-rosse. Off to the side I saw a dollar bill change hands. Apparently they had bet on which of us would lose it first. *Nice.* To be honest, for the first week or so, I was sick on each of my more than a dozen deployments. Just not like this. It took me a half hour to get it all cleaned up and even then essence of puke filled the air. I'm hoping, gentle reader, you weren't midway through breakfast while reading this but it was what it was.

Our LPO was able to scrounge up some large trash bags and twine and we settled back in- rolling chairs tied to the rack, us tied to the chairs, and the trash bags looped around our necks. Arms extended past the trash bags to our now sticky keyboards, we did our duty. And that's how it was for a week. We ate only saltine crackers with a little water to wash it down. At work we wanted to hurl. In our racks we wanted to hurl. And gripping the sides of the toilet bowls I had to clean as part of collateral duty, I wanted to hurl. But we persevered. And everyone who has ever served knows our mantra- *Duty, Honor, Country.* We did our duty to respect the honor of the committed sailors who came before us. That honorable act served our country. Our country needed and deserved our duty; plain and simple. *Puke be damned.*

Stealthily embedded in the northward-bound storm, we remained undetected for over four days. Early in the morning of the fifth day, somewhere off New York City, the storm turned eastward leaving behind a thick fog. Through it we crept, pretending to be just part of the normal merchant traffic. And then one by one we targeted them all. *VICTORY!*

Excitement filled the ship as we steamed to for Halifax for liberty. The last week of July and first week of August are the peak summertime days in Nova Scotia. And with the storm gone, the weather was absolutely beautiful. Liberty time was favorable and we were each afforded two of our three days there to go exploring. On the first day we took a historical tour; learning the city's history from the beginning of Father Le Loutre's War in 1749 to the 1917 explosion of the French munitions ship SS Mont-Blanc that to that point is believed to have been the largest explosion short of a nuclear weapon, to the rebuilding of the city into a modern day metropolis.

The residents of Halifax were very cordial and there were American tourists and business people visiting too. With the exception of some funny looking money and the quaint accent of the locals it felt a lot like visiting an American city for the first time. The restaurants and night clubs were great too; excellent food and popular dance music. This is a place I'd highly recommend for a couple's get away.

Throughout our stay the mess decks treated us to steak, lobster, and ice cream. This too was part of the reward for winning the exercise. The steak and ice cream we already had aboard and the lobster, fresh and succulent, had to have been locally-caught. The naval exercise victory was a full team effort, justly earned, and had us walking tall.

Lesson: You are sometimes you are going to have to do things you don't want to do. It could be washing your parent's car, cleaning the kitchen, scrubbing the bathroom, or even puking your guts out while tied to a rolling chair in a storm for a week. Know this, when it's done you will have become a stronger person for it. There will be moments while you are toiling away that will give you the peace of mind to collect your thoughts and think about your life and your future in ways you cannot imagine. They will appear as little glimmers of insight and hope and will help you to make better plans. Embrace these opportunities for personal growth.

Channel Fever: A Cool Navy Tradition

The Tidewater area of Virginia is a beautiful place with its own distinct character. Gorgeous beaches, winding rivers, green forests teaming with wildlife, great schools, and there are plenty of things to do. And with so many bases there are military families everywhere. Two of the great things about military families are that they are all there for the same reasons and they have built connections through shared experiences. These are very patriotic, very family-oriented people who look out for each other. Like any good tribe, they get together in our off hours for fun- cook outs, dinners in, softball games, group trips up to Bush Gardens Williamsburg, and more. And whenever a friend was deployed, they stayed in touch with his family to make sure things were going well. The same is true of the single sailors- when I was in we'd have them over to our apartment regularly and especially for the holidays when they had duty and couldn't get home. Looking back, it really didn't cost much but being there for the larger Navy family was invaluable and just seemed a very natural way to live.

Similarly, sailors look out for each other at sea; keeping each other motivated and generally in a good state of mind. In the last few days of a longer deployment most sailors get so excited and worked up they just can't fall asleep. The realization you'll get to see friends, family, and for some their newly born children is oftentimes too much to take. The Navy realizes this too and formally or informally adopted a tradition around this called "Channel Fever."

Driving a large Navy ship into the Norfolk Navy Base takes some time. There is the Chesapeake Bay Bridge Tunnel to navigate around, lots of merchant and civilian traffic, and natural hazards. Leading up to it, most ships on which I served threw Channel Fever parties on the mess decks. There would be card tournaments for spades and hearts, movie marathons of everyone's favorites like Star Wars and Rocky, along with good food too. To thank the crew for its hard work, our LPOs would man the kitchens and serve up all the pizza and ice cream the crew wanted. And this would go almost all night. Sailors had their final haircuts, liberty uniforms pressed, and again and again we shared plans for the exciting things we were going to do once we pulled in.

A Navy homecoming is a sight everyone should see at least once in his life. Families put on their Sunday best outfits, make up signs, bring flowers, and gather at the pier. Sailors put on their dress uniforms and man the rails; lining up around the main deck of the ship as a way of saluting and rendering honors. As the ship pulls up to the pier the crowd goes wild- cheering, clapping, and crying. Loved ones are finally home and the feelings that envelop a person are tough to describe. If you'd like to get a real feel for it, I invite you to go to *YouTube.com* and do a simple search for "military homecomings." It's truly worth a watch.

Lesson: The old saying though is true, absence does make the heart grow fonder.

Final Mission

"Freedom is a fragile thing and is never more than one generation away from extinction. It is not ours by inheritance; it must be fought for and defended constantly by each generation..."

- President Ronald Reagan

Not every deployment is a planned event. Some are unexpected and quite the real deal. At 9 PM one Sunday night in March of 1986 I was home putzing around, doing the things most people do to prepare for the coming work week, when my Chief and LPO knocked on the apartment door. As I opened it up and let them in a wave of dread came over me as I thought, "Oh not again, bad family news isn't something I need right now." This time was different. They were here for me because I was a seasoned E-5, Petty Officer Second Class, with nearly a dozen deployments under my belt and at the absolute top of my game.

They said, "Tom, we have a special mission for you. You need to pack up, say absolutely nothing to your wife or family about where you are going, and check in on the USS Ticonderoga CG-47, by 3 AM. The ship is pulling out at 6 AM. These are your orders." "Where are we headed, Chief?" I asked. He hesitated, I didn't. Working in the Comm Center as we called it is far more interesting than watching glazed fat pills zip by at a Dunkin Doughnuts factory and I had become one of those "Type A" people who fed on information. Whispering I said, "It's Libya, isn't it." They gave a little smile and just repeated, "Keep it to yourself." "Aye, Chief" was the only correct response. All at once I was a little nervous, excited, and proud my command chose me. It was the whole point of our being there- to be a ship shape, intellectually engaged, chomping-at-the-bit, can-do sailor when the call comes. And I was.

The next couple of hours, as my heart raced, I washed and folded my gear and then stuffed my sea bag. And I did my best to be reaffirming that all would be well, yet dodged the incessant stream of questions from my wife. It was a difficult thing to do from a relationship perspective but sometimes hard choices have to be made. In retrospect, my decision to keep it quiet was small in scale when compared to the decision the Commander In Chief had to make in sending us directly into harm's way.

In January 1986, President Ronald Reagan said there was irrefutable evidence Libyan leader Moammar Gadhafi, the "Mad Dog of the Middle East", was involved in the Rome and Vienna airport attacks carried out on December 27, 1985. Seven Arab terrorists attacked the two airports with assault rifles and hand grenades; wounding over a hundred civilians and killing nineteen before four of the terrorists were killed and three captured. Around the same time Libya began the installation of SA-5 surface-to-air missile batteries and radars they had received from the Soviet Union to bolster their air defense. We were also advised the Libyans had patrol boats with Russian-made surface to surface anti-ship missiles which could easily take us out so things were getting interesting.

Mr. Gadhafi was on the bad guy list of many Western countries, so when the Libyan leader claimed the entire Gulf of Sidra was their territory and the latitudinal line at 32° 30' N was "The Line of Death" it was the last straw. Presidents Nixon, Carter, Reagan, Bush, Clinton, Bush, and even Obama each had their own way of leading. The absolute last one in the bunch one would want to *double-dog-dare* was President Reagan. Almost two years prior, on August 11, 1984, while preparing to make his weekly Saturday radio address then President Ronald Reagan made the following joke: "My fellow Americans, I'm pleased to tell you today that I've signed legislation that will outlaw Russia forever. We begin bombing in five minutes."

Now this was Russia, that Russia; the big dog at the time. Libya was little more than one of those yippy, three and a half pound mutts that jumped up and down in the background, occasionally nipping at your ankle. But enough was enough. That nipping was beginning to affect relations between countries, international commerce, and people's basic ability to travel. So as part of the USS America battle group we sailed swiftly across the Atlantic. We drilled like the Navy version of summer football two-a-day practices- constant general quarters drills and great conversations among the crypto team, the intel team, and everyone in the Combat Information Center (CIC). Everyone knew his job and how we were going to function as one. To give you an idea of the group we were sending, I had been deployed eleven times before- this time I was the most junior member of the detachment. And this time, not one chair we were given had wheels.

The USS Ticonderoga was a state of the art Aegis Guided Missile Cruiser and the lead ship in her class. Commissioned January 22, 1983, I had actually been serving in the Navy longer than she was afloat. Several of my shipmates proudly wore their "Plank Owner" ball caps; meaning they were the part of the initial crew when she was commissioned. Now to this point I'd served on many Navy ships- older frigates, cruisers, helicopter landing ships, and others. This was a little different, just a little more special. Brand new ship, many Plank Owner sailors, the most advanced gear in the world- it was almost as if the crew and ship were breathing as one. I knew I was good but the pureness of this environment inspired me to step back and think to myself, "Dayum, I need stay atop of my game."

By Tom Nicholas

The usual trip from Norfolk to the Mediterranean Sea included a quick stop in Rota, Spain and a day or so of liberty. Not this time. We headed directly for 32° 30' N; The Line Of Death. The first three ships to cross the line were the Ticonderoga, the USS Scott DDG-995, and the USS Caron DD-970. The Caron, commissioned in late 1977, was a Spruance-class destroyer named after Medal of Honor earner Hospital Corpsman Third Class Wayne M. Caron who was killed in action during the Vietnam War. She too was new, top of the line for her time, and would go on to serve during the Persian Gulf Wars. The USS Scott had an interesting back story of her own as Kidd-class destroyer ordered by the Shah of Iran. She had been equipped with heavy-duty air conditioning for better filtering of sand and the negative effects of NBC (nuclear, biological, chemical) warfare as well as other enhancements. In the fleet we jokingly referred to her as an "Ayatollah-class" guided missile destroyer due to the understanding Iran had ordered her and after the Islamic revolution President Reagan did a "Yeah, no. We're going to just keep her.." *meaning we sure as hell didn't want to face her.*

On March 24th at 06:00, USS Ticonderoga, accompanied by the USS Scott and USS Caron, moved south of the "Line", covered by fighter aircraft. Although we are still under obligation not to go into deeper operational details, even thirty year old ones, it is now public knowledge our total team effort resulted in multiple Libyan patrol boats being sunk and their air force being completely thwarted. Navy Admiral and then chairman of the Joint Chiefs of Staff William James Crowe, Jr. stated in a post action press conference, "I frankly would have to rate it in my professional judgment as a flawless operation."

Wikipedia has an excellent synopsis of the encounter; search Action_in_the_Gulf_of_Sidra_(1986).

After the mission we sailed northwest to Augusta, Sicily; childhood home to my immigrant great grandparents. Pulling into port it felt as if we'd just won the Super Bowl. Service members completely filled the pier and the crews of the ships tied up next to us were all clapping and cheering like crazy. We felt honored, appreciated, and loved all at once. Wow. This is what they mean when they say, "We are one big family."

For a day or so we discussed and debriefed on what we'd done, how we might have done anything differently or better, and what was to come. Eventually I'd fly back to Norfolk and rejoin my unit, however, this final mission was the perfect culmination to all the training, experience, and big-brother kind of advice I'd received from my LPOs and Chief Vohland.

Lesson: The concepts I've learned through the Navy-way of team building are ones I've carried and utilized to this day. They have helped me build, lead, and mentor several successful software engineering teams, earn a good living, and provide for my family. I invite everyone to consider serving in the United States Military. It's easily the best win-win for you and the country. You may even choose to make a career of it.

Closing the loop from a different angle, today more than ever I feel one of the most challenging jobs in the world must be that of leading a North African country like Libya. On the one hand there are millions of citizens who have seen some of Western civilization either in person or online and are intrigued as to how freedom and gender equality could actually work- that women could develop and use their brains, intuition, courage, and determination as well as men do- resulting in positive societal outcomes. And that all people, regardless of race, gender, age, and other factors are free to pursue their life dreams and be happy without fear of oppression. On the other hand there are millions of Muslims very much invested in continuing and extending the reach of their culture as derived from the teachings in the Holy Quran. And some of the more conservative ones believe society runs best when citizens more-strictly follow original teachings. The dichotomy between these views is self-evident and my intent is not to solve this challenge many African and Middle Eastern leaders face; merely to highlight it. If you offered me the job of leading Libya, I wouldn't touch it with a ten foot pole.

Letter Of Commendation

Towards the end of my service as a Cryptologic Technician and prior to the last mission I was honored to have earned two letters of commendation from the Commander, Naval Security Group. Receiving even one is a rare event and this is what the last one read:

The Commander, Naval Security Group Command
takes pleasure in commending
Cryptologic Technician Third Class Thomas W. Nicholas
United States Navy
for service as set forth in the following
Citation

For outstanding performance of duty while serving as a member of surface Cryptologic Direct Support Elements in support of Commander in Chief, U.S. Atlantic Fleet from August 1983 to April 1986. Embarked for twelve deployments accumulating over 300 days at sea, you met every challenge with exceptional motivation. Your knowledge of tactical Special Intelligence Communications contributed greatly to the success of direct support missions, and your outstanding spirit of cooperation was inspirational to your shipmates. In real-world cryptologic mission and exercises, you exceeded expectations to achieve the highest standards of professional performance. Your outstanding motivation, superior performance and dedication to duty reflect great credit upon yourself, the Naval Security Group, and the United States Navy. WELL DONE!

D.H. McDowell
Rear Admiral, U. S. Navy

Just prior to receiving this second letter of commendation I was also promoted to E-5, Petty Officer Second Class. There were very few mistakes I made during my Naval service but I think it could be valuable to let you know the one most on my mind today. The USS Ticonderoga earned the Navy Expeditionary Medal on this mission. Other ships on which I'd served for multiple months also earned awards. My mistake was not having those TAD orders entered into my service record. With the exception of the aforementioned letters of commendation there may be little evidence they exist. Cryptologic Technicians only deploy when it's critical to the success of the mission. If you are fortunate to serve in the military, someday after serving you may also wish to join your local chapter of the Veterans Of Foreign Wars (VFW). So make sure everything you do is entered into your permanent service record- they will need this information in order to welcome you aboard.

And Now His Watch Is Ended

Service in the military is exactly what you make it; as is pretty much everything in life. Speaking with a voice of experience, I'm here to tell you every situation represents an opportunity to learn regardless of whether or not you have fully bought into what it is you are doing. When you look at things that way, life will become a lot more fun and you'll get much more out of it.

The leadership and technical training the Navy provides is the best. They have been doing this for hundreds of years and the maturity of process shows in everything they do. At first it's all new, then you start to see the sense in it, and finally you're all in.

The saying, "See the world, join the Navy" was definitely true for me. There were some outstanding port calls- the lush jungles near Roosevelt Roads, Puerto Rico; the snow-blanketed fjords near Trondheim, Norway; the afternoon sun hitting the buildings in Madrid, Spain, the beautiful views from the Baha garden in Haifa, Israel; the teaming wildlife of the Panama Canal; and the hospitality and culture of Acapulco, Mexico. As a young man in my twenties, there was no way I could have afforded all these trips as vacations, yet they were a free benefit of serving in the United States Navy.

My preferred, stateside shore tour was coming to an end. My rating or job was manned at one hundred six percent, meaning we had more sailors than were needed as CTs. The fact I'd deployed so many times and done so with distinction made the Navy want to keep me. I was offered pretty much any overseas duty station I wanted; England, Hawaii, Italy, Japan, or a ship home ported overseas. During this time I had also been paying into the Navy's college tuition plan. So I was torn.

Spending so much time at sea also provided the opportunity to read and one of the books I stumbled across has inspired me for the last two decades: *"Think And Grow Rich"* by Napoleon Hill. Working for a national business magazine and writing a series on successful men, Napoleon Hill was sent to interview early American steel industrialist Andrew Carnegie. The interview yielded the secrets Carnegie used to control his own thinking and thereby pursue his vision of the American Dream. Hill also interviewed famous and successful early Americans such as Henry Ford, Alexander Graham Bell, Thomas Edison, Harvey Firestone, Theodore Roosevelt, Charles Schwab, John Wanamaker, and F.W. Woolworth. The sum of all these lessons is neatly organized and laid out in such a way anyone could come up with a personal plan for success to achieve virtually anything he desired.

In the book Hill provides inspiration for personal motivation, tips on organizing and creating a plan for success, identification of the fears that hold most people back and supportive tactics for overcoming those fears. Many real-life anecdotes from people who overcame overwhelming adversity to realize their vision of the American Dream are also included. The one thing they all had in common was not the number of setbacks- it was that they never, ever gave up. I very much recommend you read this book. His insights are as helpful today as they were the day the book was written and millions of successful people have already benefited from his wisdom. You can too.

Another outstanding book with useful, practical tips is Dale Carnegie's *"How To Win Friends And Influence People."* This one teaches people how to make new friends quickly and easily, how to win people to your way of thinking, and improve your ability to get things done. It also prepares people to become better diplomats in handling complaints and avoiding arguments in the first place. Carnegie's book also offers great tips for improved communications with others.

The United States Navy had transformed me from a somewhat unsure man with lots of energy into a highly motivated one with keen focus. I wasn't one hundred percent sure what I wanted to do but I was sure no matter the choice, I would succeed. Having been recently been promoted to Petty Officer Second Class, I was looking at four years of duty before I'd even be eligible to take the ratings exam for Petty Officer First Class; the next rank up. Recognizing my "Type A" personality and being a man of action, I couldn't accept the idea of cooling my heels in the same job for that long. At the same time, the world of computing was just beginning to bloom and although unstated in the earlier Final Mission chapter of this book, prior to leaving Norfolk on the USS Ticonderoga someone had provided we CTs with two new, in-the-box, Zenith desktop computers. They said, "Here, take these too. You might be able to use them."

About two days out to sea while steaming towards Libya, I'd opened the boxes, set up one of the desktop computers, and was ravenously consuming all its documentation. Given it was brand new government property and might somehow benefit our mission, I was being very careful not to misconfigure or mishandle it. Once it was all connected I powered it up and a simple screen popped up asking the user to input the current time in a specific format. I followed the format exactly. Result: An error message that would let me go no further yet included the option to try again. I clicked it and carefully reentered the time in the correct format. Same problem.

I rebooted the computer, tried again and again and again. Still the same issue. At first I thought I'd done something to break it. Then I realized that wasn't the case and came to see this as opportunity. The personal computing industry was in its infancy. This was the spring of 1986. I really enjoyed working with computers and solving puzzles and I began to wonder if there were computer jobs out there. Fast forward to being home now, after the mission, I recalled this event and went out to buy the closest national newspaper, The Washington Post.

Although only the Wednesday edition, there were seven or eight pages of computer jobs; programmers, analysts, database architects, and more. It made me wonder what the larger, Sunday edition would hold. This was before the internet and all its really cool job websites. Impatiently I waited, and then the big day came. As soon as I woke up I raced to our local 7-11 convenience store and picked up the voluminous Sunday Washington Post. Oh.. my.. God. There were over thirty pages of computer jobs. Every type of private company and government agency was represented; large, medium, and small. And they were competing for people to do work I already thought was interesting. All this advertising meant two things:

1. This was a rapidly growing area of employment.

2. There was a shortage of people able to do it- meaning one could earn enough in this career to support himself and a family.

As an aside but related to the idea of choosing a major, I highly recommend people check out Aaron Clary's book, *"Worthless: The Young Person's Indispensable Guide to Choosing the Right Major."* As a successful engineer I can attest to the accuracy and usefulness of his writing and think it can help guide your college major decision.

After my Marion Military Institute academic debacle, the Navy had rebuilt my confidence and instilled in me the drive to excel. But did I have what was needed to take it to the next level? I thought so, I hoped so, I prayed so. But really, I didn't know about this unexplored civilian work world. So I asked my wife, my dad, and my aunts and uncles what they thought of the idea.

The responses varied. My wife, younger than me, was supportive but like me lacked factual information to help in the decision. My dad, aunts, and uncles offered a more negative response. They thought the idea was fraught with risk and couldn't understand how I would walk away from a great career in the Navy. I pointed out the ways in which the world was changing to no avail- they were stuck in their positions. And after a while I realized why and this links directly back to the earlier *Spheres Of Influence* section of the book.

My elder relatives were people whose families had survived the Great Depression of the 1930's and then World War II. They had witnessed the civil turbulence of the 1960's and distrusted the government then and into the 1970's. And they had experienced a lot of struggle and misery over the years. To them the "Yuppies," well-paid young, middle-class, professionals who work in city jobs and have luxurious lifestyles, were a fad and more likely a lie being proffered by younglings who hadn't earned the fame and fortune they were flaunting. The rougher years of their lives had sucked the zest for life, hopes, and idea of the American Dream right out of them. A few had turned to God and found a peace that helped them rebuild their lives- from ground zero to about thirty miles out; the maximum distance they were willing to travel from their homes. Others had turned to spending their waning years watching cable TV news 24x7 and seemed to be waiting for society to break down and implode upon itself. Collectively, they had lost that innocence and spirit of adventure we all have when we are younger. I still had it, just as you probably do today, and I was willing to build on the lessons I'd learned to this point and continue onward. For me, the adventure was still just beginning.

There were some jobs I could take on with the Navy experience I had accumulated. However, to be really prepared for a career of the future a college degree was required. Most of the dozens of pages of technology jobs required a degree in computer science or electrical engineering. They weren't looking for degrees in history or communications- the burgeoning field was and remains engineering and it requires a solid math and science background. Back then we mostly used the public library to obtain information, so that's where I went to research Old Dominion and Norfolk State- the two larger universities in our area with computer science programs.

Old Dominion University was less than a mile from my apartment complex and some of her students lived nearby. These kids were generally nice, focused, and not as rowdy as I expected ones that age to be. One day I did a self-tour of the campus. Walking there I noticed beautiful and elegant, southern-style homes with bright white columns and large front porches dotting the neighborhood. The campus buildings, courtyards, and sidewalks were clean and well maintained. I then found the Department Of Computer Science and began reading the bulletin boards and schedules. Finding one of the Introduction to Computer Science classrooms, I gave it a peek. Wow- the place was packed. It was an auditorium style class with well over one hundred students. There were a couple graduate assistants in the room and the professor was at the front speaking. Was this how all classes at Old Dominion were going to be? And what chance would there be of communicating with the professor should I have a question? From this limited perspective it didn't look good. If I was going to pay for an education I wanted to consume every bit of it. And then I looked at the price. For me, a twenty-four year old emancipated from his parents with little to no money, Old Dominion University just wasn't affordable.

On to Norfolk State! NSU was about four miles from my home but still an acceptable commute; even by bike if the car were to break down. It too looked nice and well maintained. One difference I noticed immediately was everyone was so friendly. They looked at you, smiled, and said, "Hello." Being from New Jersey, a place where one is equally likely to receive a visceral grunt and a head-nod as he is to have someone offer a greeting, this was a bit of a changeup. But I liked it.

Having been priced out of ODU I decided to cut to the chase and make the admissions office my first stop. I needed to know if I could afford to attend before getting excited about the major or the school. Tuition at Norfolk State University was significantly lower than at Old Dominion and I quickly determined I would be able to afford three semesters. Then when I went to ask a lady in Admissions a question, a big old grin came across her face. "Oh honey we've got a minority grant just for you" she said. What? Minority grant? Turns out the drive for diversity went both ways. If you happened to be a white student attending a traditionally black university you qualified for a minority grant of $500 per semester for four semesters. My hope of earning a degree was suddenly gaining some traction.

All this having been written, I needed to come up with a better financial plan. My Navy time at sea had enabled me to bank seventy-two days of paid leave. This meant I could use the vacation time and take on a second job. For the next almost three months I ended my navy tour on leave; while working the night shift at two neighborhood 7-11 stores. One was in the more preppy ODU neighborhood and the other was in a very poor, predominantly black one on the other side of town. Patrons of both locations gave me odd looks for very different reasons. The preppy kids regularly mocked me as a twenty-something underachiever and the poorer people looked at me a little funny when I'd say, "Yes sir" and "Yes mam" when making their coffee. But my parents raised me right- *you be nice to everyone.* And as for the mockery- *it only served to motivate me.*

My wife at the time worked as a clerk for a construction company and the United States Navy added a little more to the budget when I agreed to remain in the Reserves. The Reserve money for an E-5 was an additional $265 per month and it meant a lot.

Leaving the Navy was one of the more difficult decisions I had made to that point in my life. These were my friends, my family, and they'd really been there for me and me for them. Getting in my car and driving off the base for the last time, at least twice I took my foot off the gas pedal, coasted for a bit, and wanted to turn around and reenlist. It hurt a lot. But sometimes, you have to take a leap of faith. And I did.

By Tom Nicholas

PART IV: BEHOLD, THE GREEN & GOLD: A WHITE MALE'S PERSPECTIVE ON ATTENDING A HISTORICALLY BLACK COLLEGE

Being a student at Norfolk State University was my first real exposure to a larger college. And until this time I didn't even realize historically black colleges existed. But here I have a confession to make; kind of a bad one. My grades at Marion Military Institute were poor- so poor in fact that had I applied to NSU with those transcripts they would have never accepted me. So I took a very big risk and didn't tell them. I applied as a true freshman, eager and willing to start all over and I prayed I'd get just one more chance. Now I'm not sure if it was because this was pre-internet or because colleges are truly just businesses that sell enlightenment, however, they accepted me. Deep breath- here went nothing and at the same time, everything.

You Don't Have The Guts To Shave My Head

Working the night shift at 7-11 in June and July of 1986 meant I had some free time during the day to explore the Norfolk State campus and to see what was what. The school had several newer class buildings, a bunch of older ones which looked like they'd been around since the 1950's, a big student union building, nice field house, practice football and baseball fields, and everything else one would hope to see. However, in the summer time the place was virtually empty. Walking around and looking somewhat lost I was approached by a taller, thin gentleman sporting pressed slacks and a sharp, white polo shirt. "Son, can I help you find something on campus?" were the first words spoken to me by my new friend and future mentor, Coach Tom Morris.

"No sir, I'm just looking around a little early," I said. Without missing a beat he replied, "Football doesn't start for another week son. We haven't met before. Are you planning to be a walk on?"

Football? From there Coach invited me into his office to meet and get to know each other. We talked about the school, my academic plans, time in the Navy, and the football program. I could have played linebacker, maybe even some defensive end, but I wasn't on scholarship and didn't want to risk a physical injury that could prevent me from working the night shift at 7-11 or making my monthly Navy Reserve duty. Those things were putting food on the table and I needed to be careful. Two things I could do were kick and punt; especially punt. Yeah, I know, a punter-big whup. But like anything else it's a matter of perspective. Punters only get on the field a few times a game. But on each of those plays they touch the ball. What they do can swing an entire battle one way or the other. And a few times in the coming season they certainly did.

Thanking Coach Morris for his time, I said I'd be back in a week ready to rock. For the next several days I took my football over to the Old Dominion football stadium, the then home for Norfolk State's games, and kicked and kicked. It was hot and humid every day. However, I'd punt and chase that one ball up and down the field time and time again. And once again, a leap of faith was about to pay off.

On the first day of football tryouts there were over one hundred players out there and two of them also wanted the punting job. First we had to do a two mile run. After about four laps around the football field I heard one coach say to another, "That's the Navy guy." On the next lap, excited at simply being there and hyperventilating, I projectile vomited- chunks of my breakfast almost hitting another player. I stopped for a second, goopy saliva dripping onto my plastic K-Mart cleats, and then got going again as fast as I could. The same coach then told another one, "Military guys just don't quit." A few minutes later the run was complete and hurl-and-all I met the time needed for a punter- which was, unbeknownst to me, basically not tripping over yourself.

Over the next two weeks we ran and kicked and kicked and ran. We had team meetings, meals together, and I continued talking with Coach Morris. And each day the academic information I withheld weighed upon me like a five hundred pound blocking sled; making me feel counterfeit and unworthy. So I worked harder and harder- almost punishing myself for the lie of omission. Coach and others on the team just saw me as driven and until now, in this book, I've never told anyone. I didn't want to be auto ejected from school nor did I want to put Coach Morris in the position of protecting me. Between you and me, never ever put yourself in this kind of position. It's not a mentally healthy place to be.

Finally the day came. The team was about to announce who made the cut and who would go to the practice squad. The three of us were still there and had to compete on the dirt practice field, with a long snapper, in front of everyone. The first guy shanked two of his first three punts and was invited to step aside. Then it came down to me and the last guy. He also played another position; safety. Although a sophomore he was pretty good at both positions. The previous year's starting punter had graduated though so this was a wide open competition.

Our first two punts were relatively even. Then he shanked one. We could begin to hear the other players react with "Ooooh.." My next one was a rocket, going a good 60 yards. There was silence. His next one was a warped looking knuckle ball going about 35 yards. He was feeling the pressure and I was starting to feel a little more relaxed. My fourth one was another rocket going about the same distance with a good spiral. The other players liked it. Coach Morris said, "Okay, one more. Give it your best and remember, hang time matters." This time my competitor got off a decent and respectable kick, probably 45 yards. Feeling almost exhilarated, I just smiled and put my hands out. Perfect snap, perfect drop, and another beastly kick; this time very high with an outstanding hang time. The job was mine.

After practice we got cleaned up and had to make our way to that night's meeting where they were to announce the team. While I was excited at the prospect of making the team I was also dreading the initiation. For more than a week several strong upper classmen had been giving me that what-are-you-doing-here look. Initiation consisted of having your hair buzz cut and then the frightening mystery of whatever else football players willing to wallow in mud could think up. Walking into the meeting it felt the way popular culture describes a person's first day in prison.

The story goes, you either need to pick a fight with the strongest guy or become someone's punk.

As I walked into the meeting most of the players and coaches were already there. One of the seniors, a tall, strong, lean looking defensive back and likely team captain, was sitting down in the middle of the first row. Tossing the possibility of his frightening reaction to the winds, I walked up to him and just stared- not saying a word. He looked up at me. I then gave him a Star Trek Klingon-style grunt of derision. That, he didn't like. At this point the stadium-style meeting room grew quiet and people were taking notice.

"What the hell do you want?" he snarled.

Not missing a beat I looked him up and down and said, "You don't have the guts to shave my head!"

As you'd expect this was met with a huge roar of "Ooooooh!" from the other players.

He just smiled, nodded, and said, "Sit your ass down. When this is over, you're mine."

The players grinned and the coaches did too. The official team was then announced, meeting wrapped up, and the coaches told everyone to play nice and make sure we got plenty of sleep for the next day's practice. At that point the team captain grabbed me by the bottom of my ear like I was an errant seven year old and walked me completely across campus to the dorms. Everyone followed.

In front of them all, top to bottom, left to right, and even swirling the clippers, he gave me a really good baldy haircut as the rest of the team cheered. And you know what? From then on we were friends, I was part of the team, and nobody messed with me.

Being a white guy on the Norfolk State University football team is you know what? Not really any different from the friendship and teammate perspective of being on any other team. Guys talked football, women, what they were going to do for dinner any given night, and all the normal things guys talk about. One big difference though was music.

Growing up in South Jersey with my friend and Middle Township High School football team mate, Jay, Van Halen and rock music like that was our go-to. In 1986 I'd just seen the Van Hagar 5150 concert and was wearing out the cassette in my beat-to-crap 1967 Plymouth Valiant. For all the younger readers, feel free to Google "cassette tape." It was a plastic, less durable device we used to hold our music but it worked well enough. Norfolk State away game bus music was anything but rock. Back then, the team listened to the rap of LL Cool J', Doug E. Fresh & Slick Rick, and Eric B. Several games into the season I decided to reaffirm our friendship. Remember the earlier part of this book, in the Navy section where I wrote the only mess with you if they like you? Well, advance this story a few games into the season and now it was my time to step up and play that *mess-with-ya* role.

We were travelling by bus from Norfolk, Virginia to the city of Charlotte, North Carolina for a game versus the Golden Bears of Johnson C. Smith University. On the way down we stopped at a McDonald's to grab lunch. To lighten things up I waited till all the guys got off the bus and swapped one of their rap cassettes with one I didn't mind losing- Barry Manilow's Greatest Hits. After eating, we re-boarded the bus and continued our trek down I-95. Someone shortly yelled out, "Hey, cut the music back on." Within seconds the toe-tapping tone rang-out , "Her name was Lola. She was a showgirl. With yellow feathers in her hair.. at the Copa.. Copa Cabana..." Fifty plus sets of eyeballs turned immediately and directly upon me, and I then got to see a cassette tape skip about twenty times down I-95. So, if you happen to be in North Carolina, somewhere between Hillsborough and Mebane, keep an eye out- and run that sucker over one more time for good measure. We all got a good laugh out of it and Coach Morris just smiled and shook his head; recognizing it as a quality bonding moment.

Now on to Johnson C. Smith University and the game. It had rained on and off throughout the afternoon and into the evening but football is football and rain and mud are just *features*. To punters though, they aren't good ones. The ground is slippery making it difficult to plant your foot; and easy to pull a groin muscle when trying to kick. And the ball becomes heavily-soaked with water.

Things were going so well in school and with football I felt inspired and was taking things up a notch. After I'd punt the ball I'd run down the field like a Viking with my hair on fire looking for someone to hit. It worked pretty well in several games, until I whacked the wrong defensive guy in the first quarter of this game. For the rest of the game he and a buddy of his targeted me every time I headed down field and man did they clock me- laying me out flat several times. At one point the coach told me ease up so I'd be able to keep playing. To this day I consider the Golden Bears of Johnson C. Smith to be the hardest hitting team I've ever faced.

Lesson: If you are going to dish it out, you better be prepared to take it. It's only fair.

But of all of them, this wasn't the most interesting game. That one was to come against Morgan State University in Baltimore, Maryland. In 1986 the Morgan State University Bears held the ignominious distinction of having the nation's longest losing streak in Division II football. It was at twenty-nine games and there were seniors who hadn't experienced the thrill of a single victory. They had scheduled us for their homecoming and were hoping this would be their big chance. It was a beautiful, sunny afternoon that day and they had invited several additional marching bands to play along in support. Some looked like college bands and some looked like high school ones. ESPN was there and the master of ceremonies if you will was the 121st Mayor Of Philadelphia, Mr. Wilson Goode. The place was packed and they seemed to have brought all manner of good juju in their favor. We knew of their record and all week we were reminded by our coaches we didn't want to go down in history as the team everyone saw on ESPN who helped Morgan State get off the schneid.

There was one stadium player entrance and exit area and prior to warm ups I decided it was time to have a little fun. I stood near the opening and just hung out. Sure enough an older, local gentleman sporting a Morgan State University wind breaker approached me to say hello, size me up, and try to get into my head.

"Great day for a game. Have you ever played before so many people? By the way, what position do you play?" he asked.

I was 6' 1" tall and a svelte 250 pounds. Holding my head low, I tilted it back and forth and said, "Punter. I'm too small to play anyplace else."

At that point, shoulders slumped, the old man ambled off. *Nice try, pops.* To this day I feel a little bad for kicking it right back to him. However, although noteworthy, the encounter was not portentous. Morgan State gave us the fight of our lives.

For three quarters we fought back and forth, each team bending but not breaking. With just a little bit of time left in the fourth we were leading by a couple points but our drive had stalled and we had to punt. To this point I'd done well but the pressure was on. There was plenty of time for Morgan Sate to drive close enough to attempt a game-winning field goal. Deep breath again- I got into position. Perfect snap, perfect drop, perfect launch. Fortunately for us their punt returner misjudged the ball and it sailed over his head; bouncing on the five and slowly trickling into the end zone. It went fifty-seven yards and was my career best. The Bears got the ball on their twenty and drove it to mid field. It was at this point our Spartan defense held and through a great team effort we dodged a bullet, winning 23-21.

On some level anyone with an ounce of sportsmanship in him feels sympathy pains for a team going so long without a win. To their credit, Morgan State stood up and made a real fight of it. Painful as it may seem, the experience built character in those young men and they would eventually go on to earn a win against the University of the District of Columbia later that season.

Lesson: Being famous is better than being infamous, however, being a positive team player is the most important thing of all. When the team gets the "W" everyone wins. And when the team doesn't get the "W," there are always takeaways and lessons for the next time.

An Unusual Source For Scholarship Money

Football at Norfolk State was becoming an amazing experience. However, I was taking six classes, working the night shift at 7-11, and trying to help out around the house. I was so busy there was no time to get into the usual college-student kind of trouble. The first semester I earned straight A's- taking Introduction to Computer Science, a Math class, English, a History class, Physics and its accompanying lab, and the university-required Student Orientation course. Wednesdays the Physics lab made me late for football practice and the first two times I had to stay late and run extra sprints- till I explained it. The second semester was similar and it brought my first programming course in Fortran in addition to a second course in Physics.

The schedule felt torturous. School, football, study, work, a little time to sleep and then it all repeated. Week night working I'd take my books in with me to the 7-11. From 1 AM till 4 AM, few if any customers would come in in and I could study. Weekends were a little better but not much and I was starting to stress over next year's school funding. It was going to run out unless I found another option. Combine the schedule and the stress and I ended up getting one B in the second semester. I know this will sound crazy but that one B grade and the lack of money made me consider dropping out to become an interstate truck driver. I had read they made pretty good money and a local trucking school was looking for candidates. Additionally, I had visited Norfolk State's placement office. Their mission was to help students find employment after graduation as well as internships. Again, virtually out of money I had become desperate.

The internship process involved filling out a bunch of paperwork, preparing a resume, and obtaining four letters of recommendation from professors or other professionals with whom one had worked. Since my grades were good, I went to my computer science professors, my math professor, and my history professor. Those were my best and most favorite classes and my hard work paid off. They each wrote fantastic letters highlighting my hard work and potential. I was so happy to have the letters I made copies of them all- and later I would be happy I did.

That summer I took on a daytime construction laborer job, helping to rehab an old building. It was hard, dirty, hands on, tedious and tiresome work. I only owned two pairs of cheaper, K-Mart blue jeans and this job had destroyed them both. After the construction site day shift I'd come home, wash up, grab something to eat, try to sew up the holes in my jeans, and then go work the night shift at 7-11. Shockingly on one of the night shifts a few of the Navy Crypto sailors with whom I'd served, including one very hot woman fully resistant to my natural charm, came into the 7-11. As they made their purchases she recognized me, giggled, and made a comment about my prospects not improving. Little did she know, little did she know. One takes his motivation from wherever it comes and her persistent degradation fueled the fire-for-achievement in me beyond description.

I knew there were financial scholarships here and there- football, Navy and Army ROTC, and maybe more. My first stop back on campus was the Computer Science Department. I wanted to say hello to my advisor, Dr. George Harrison and learn more about our local chapter of the Association For Computing Machinery (ACM); a professional organization for computer scientists and engineers. Dr. Harrison and I really clicked. It was impressive he had earned his Ph.D. in Mathematics from the University of Virginia as well as a Masters in Computer Science from Old Dominion University. I had never met a more learned and established man. Perhaps once one reaches a certain level in life, call it maturity, call it natural personality, call it tenure, it becomes a little easier to smile while imparting wisdom. He was there. And I was just beginning the journey.

After our friendly chat I decided to take a look on the bulletin board outside the department's office. And there it was- on a single sheet of white paper with university letterhead. The McDaniel Jones Mathematics scholarship program was soliciting applications. Two students who had full rides, four years of academic scholarship money, had apparently washed out and the remainder of their funds were available. The scholarships were for full tuition but not books, fees, or anything else. Quickly I chatted up the department's administrative assistant to obtain an application. How would I compare to the other applicants? I wasn't sure. We started the year with an estimated three hundred (300) freshman majoring in computer science. So there was a lot of potential competition.

There were a myriad of factors going into this equation. It was a traditionally black university so I respected the importance of their mission; especially the hopefulness that comes to a nation upon seeing more minority engineers. On the flip side I helped them check a few equality boxes myself being a white minority on this campus and a Navy veteran. I was also a starter on the university football team and on the Dean's list both of my first semesters. Then it dawned on me. Devious? Unusual? Almost not fair? Or was it perfectly within my right? Along with the scholarship application I included the letters of recommendation; some of them written by professors in my department who happened to sit on the scholarship selection board.

About a month later a letter came to my home: Norfolk State University is happy to advise you have been selected for the McDaniel Jones Mathematics scholarship. I'd earned full tuition for the remainder of my undergraduate degree. Including adhering to the university's student code of conduct I needed to maintain at least a 3.0/4.0 GPA. The weight of paying tuition had been completely lifted off my chest. What a relief. It also put into full perspective my focus needed to be more about protecting my academic scholarship and less about football.

As the fall semester and football season approached I prepared for camp. Football practices started in August and late summer in Norfolk, Virginia was its usual hot and humid self. This kind of weather is awesome if you're chilling out on Virginia Beach. In downtown Norfolk on a football field, not so much. Two-a-day practices again started at 6 AM. Even then it was in the upper 70's and the grass wet with dew. We ran, we did up-downs, and busted our collective keisters till we were dirt-coated masses of dripping sweat. Although a returning starter, I had competition and one of the guys was pretty good. He was so good in fact when the season started the team kept two punters the first two games.

I had worked hard to become a college starter; one of the things a lot of boys dream of when they're ten years old. Living that dream, I felt like an overjoyed kid again. Each week was full of excitement. Our coaches worked us hard and we continued to give them everything we had. We attended our meetings, watched ESPN's coverage of college games, followed the standings, and more. And each weekend we donned our armor, the stellar-looking Norfolk State Spartan green and gold, and were ready for battle. Sure we were a Division II school but in our hearts and minds each one of us was that scrappy kid from the movie, "Rudy," and we wanted a piece of everyone and anyone.

The week before one of our games I experienced an event that would change my outlook towards football completely. One of our better running backs blew out his knee and was done. Done-done. I had watched him get carted off the field but there were so many people around him I couldn't get close enough to wish him well. The following Tuesday I came across him on a campus bench, sitting completely alone and sobbing. Head down and not wanting to look up he had devolved into a spiritually broken man-child with no idea what to do next. His scholarship was running out and his grades were not great because he'd put all his efforts into football. To top it off his major was communications. Now some communications majors thrive in the real world, however, in the employment section I hadn't seen even one listing for a job requiring that major. From that moment on, one thought kept racing through my mind, "What if it were me?" I had come so far academically and in my ability to manage my time. I owed a lot to my parents for the way they brought me up, my 4-H leaders for the character they helped instill in me, and the U.S. Navy for helping turn me into a man.

Walking away from my teammate, my shoulders began to sink and a visceral, gut wrenching truth began to set in. As much as I loved college football, I had plans requiring the full use of my brain. For the next few days at practice I wasn't myself. I was hesitant and didn't get as many booming kicks off as usual. We went into the Saturday game sharing the punting duties. Some games you get a lot of chances, some games very few. That night I only got two. The first kick was blocked, partially due to a poor snap. The second one was a thirty-something yard knuckleball and my coach just shook his head.

The Monday after the game he called me in to ask what was up. I explained everything to him and he said, "Shake it off, son. We've seen you do a really great job here. If you perform the way you did last season, we can get you a tryout with the Green Bay Packers." Now that made me smile. Playing in the Pros was almost a fantasy. It was something which seemed impossible. These days I think him saying it was more to get me back on track, however, what I said next was the beginning of the end of my football career. "What if I end up paralyzed?" As soon as I said it I knew I'd lost my edge. And so did Coach Morris.

Later in the week our coaches named my competitor the lone starter for the upcoming game and I was moved to the practice squad. Right or wrong, I felt disowned and abandoned. Disgruntled, I spent the next week working out with the linebackers just so I could hit someone. But truthfully, my heart just wasn't in it. Being benched after being a starter was something I'd never experienced and my decision became obvious. I met again with my coach and let him know I was going to focus fully on academics, using family responsibilities, the U.S. Navy, and anything except concern of a future-jeopardizing injury to help him accept my decision. Deep down, taking this logical path was an emotional punch in the gut. But it was the right choice for me.

There would be no more team huddles, no more sucking dirt into my teeth during up-downs, no more dew filled grass at sunrise, no more screaming like a Viking with his hair on fire while running down the field, and no more chances to wear the Green and Gold. So I buried myself in my school work, my 7-11 night shift job, and Navy Reserves duty trying hard to forget or at least move on.

Some people say that when faced with a difficult decision you should always follow your heart. In this case I followed my head and based on my life over the past twenty years I can say without reservation it was the right decision. Had I played football, only one good thing might have happened. I might have earned my starting spot back. But a couple of bad things could have happened. I could have gotten injured, unlikely but possible. More likely the sacrifice of time for football could have made my grades suffer and cost me my academic scholarship. And scholarship, the desire for intellectual enlightenment, is the true reason a person should attend college.

Lesson: When choosing between two things think long term and go with your head. Write down pros and cons of each option but give serious consideration to the effects of the decision five or even ten years from now. You'll be happy you did.

Where Most Computer Science Majors Trip Up

Although a few hundred freshmen in my class declared themselves to be computer science majors, *four years later only twenty-six of us graduated.* There were a lot of variables playing into the statistic, however, when it came to coursework students struggled with one class more than any other.

That class was Calculus II: integrals and their inverse, differentials, derivatives, anti-derivatives, and approximating the area of curvilinear regions. It sounds complicated but it really isn't. There are a finite number of equations to understand and once you see the process of calculating things it's a piece of cake. The trick in this course isn't the calculus; it's remembering how to do algebra. In order to manipulate equations a solid understanding of Algebra is required.

Practicing math is free. It costs you nothing, nada, zip. A great, free, online resource for understanding math concepts is the Khan Academy; *KhanAcademy.org*. In Calculus I you learn to take the derivative of a function. In Calculus II you go the other way around- given the derivative of a function, you come up with a possible original function. You also learn the connection between areas under curves, integrals and anti-derivatives. Don't let math jargon make your eyes glaze over. Practice, practice, and then practice some more advanced algebra. Your ability to excel at calculus depends upon having a solid foundation in algebra. And algebra itself isn't that tough.

Between you and me, I lost interest in mathematics in high school when my College Prep Math instructor didn't answer my questions. He seemed to answer the questions of some other students but not mine. At that point I developed an attitude that the system was tilted to help certain students and I wasn't one of them. So I audited the class and simply gave up. If you run into a similar situation, don't go this route. Be persistent, take full advantage of the free lessons now online, and just don't give up. There is no limit to the number of times you can try and persistence denotes sincerity to an instructor. It does pay off.

Should you later develop an interest in computer science but not have the mathematics foundation or you are out of practice, it is possible to build up your skill. Simply take the foundational courses as a college freshman, schools offer these to non-science and technology majors, and then lead into majoring in computer science. It may take you an extra semester or year but I have seen students take this path and succeed.

Lesson: An ancient Chinese proverb states "The best time to plant a tree was twenty years ago. The second best time is now." The same is true with your education. Now will never come again. So start and commit now.

The Misperception Of Lost Time

One of the more inspirational things I heard my father say was something I didn't appreciate till five years after he said it. My mother had always wanted to be a nurse but set aside that dream to help provide financial support to the family. In

1980 things were looking up and she teetered back and forth about whether or not to go to college. At the dinner table she hemmed and hawed, "I'm thirty-seven. If I go it will take four years and I'll be forty." With wit and a dimpled smile my dad tilted his head and replied, "How old will you be in four years if you don't go?" She signed up the next day.

Lesson: There are a lot of different ways to realize your vision of the American Dream. When it comes to obtaining a useful college education, there is no such thing as "one right path." This is America. If you have a dream, go chase it.

Earlier in this book I wrote about false starts- trying different things and finding your way. The difference in focus and maturity between most eighteen year old college students and those in their twenties and beyond can be dramatic. As a twenty-four year old U. S. Navy veteran and freshman attending Norfolk State University I felt a little funny sitting in class with a bunch of relative younglings. I'd been to the Arctic Circle, roasted in the heat off Honduras' Tiger Island during the Nicaraguan revolution, patrolled off Beirut on a Marine amphibious assault ship, and had surface to surface missile radar locked on my ship off of Libya. So any thought of stress related to sitting in a college classroom would have been, how do you say, "cute."

Grinning from ear to ear and almost giggling to myself, I sat in my first of four Physics classes and listened to the under-nineteen crowd of kids talk about how much alcohol they drank the previous weekend and the location of next week's party. The only things on my mind were the cool concepts the professor was about to convey. I'd seen little military objects blow up bigger objects and big military objects be more agile than I'd ever imagined. Our physics professor was going to show us the baseline concepts and math behind how all that was possible.

Beer? Sure, I learned about beer in the service too but the few extra years of Navy experience really helped open my mind to what I was about to see- *in the classroom.*

Be The Curve Breaker

When grading a test on a "curve", the professor scales the grades so the student with the highest score in the class gets 100%. The grades of the other students are computed as a percentage off that. If the highest grade was an 80, for example, that becomes the "A." If a student were to pull a 72 he could still receive a "B." Nice for the student pulling a 72 but completely disingenuous with respect to what was learned. Oh, it's a "B"! Umm, no. Everyone, including the recipient, knows it's really a "D."

On August 30, 2011, Jack Moore of *Buzzfeed.com* wrote a piece titled, "The 12 Most Annoying Types Of College Students." The first in his list of annoyers is The Curve Breaker- the hard studying student who scores so well that there isn't much if any of a curve. Jack stated Curve Breakers do this to make others fail, they judge those who miss class, they suck up to the teacher, and everyone hates this kid. However, Jack only tells half the skewed story.

Only a self-righteous jerk judges others in a demeaning way. And professor's Suck-Up Radars are well tuned to those who would do that. Professors aren't fools. And with respect to getting good grades, to quote a modern day axiom, "Haters gonna hate." Some other students dislike the Curve Breaker- let me tell you why. Curve Breakers bring to light two things. First, some of the students completely understood the lessons. And second, the effort put in by the low-scoring students shows they didn't study.

Let's set the classroom perceptions aside and look at the bigger picture. You know who else loves Curve Breakers? Employers. Employers love job seekers who were Curve Breakers.

If you were looking at the resumes of two engineers and one of them earned a grade point average (GPA) of 3.75 and the other pulled a GPA of 2.12, which would you want on your team?

Over the years I've attended a few colleges and universities and applied and been accepted to a number of contracts and jobs. These are a few of the Curve Breaker benefits I've realized over the years:

- Many times professors have said, 'If you have an "A" going into the end of the term you don't have to take the final exam." They usually didn't mention this until the week before the final but it happened many times in different schools. And not having to take a test in one subject, frees a person to study for another class for which he does have to test.

- Many students competed for summer internship opportunities. Grades were a major factor in my earning internships at General Electric and Bell Communications Research.

- In the fall and spring of my senior year, recruiters of Fortune 500 companies and well known government organizations came to our Norfolk State job fairs. They weeded out candidates by GPA first. Although they met with any students at the fair, they threw special receptions, parties, and dinners only for students with GPAs above a certain level. Those were the candidates they really wanted on their teams.

- Graduate schools strongly consider GPA in selecting candidates. Someday you might want to attend one. Perhaps not today but someday.

Showing up to a job interview with a low GPA is a little like going to a party underdressed. You're a little embarrassed, they are a little embarrassed, and it's something you can't fix. Did they settle for you because their organization is dysfunctional or are they doing you a favor? Either way, you don't want to be in that position.

However, when you've got the good GPA and are invited to the intellectual equivalent of "The Big Dance" it's one of the most amazing feelings you'll ever experience. That someone respects you for your mind is worth every night of study you'll do. Trust me. Please trust me in this.

This having been written, getting a "B" grade here or there isn't the end of the world. So with zero deference to Mr. Moore of Buzzfeed, do become the hard-working, humble, respectful, friendly, Curve Breaker. And if you hear students whining and complaining that there was no curve and they're looking with derision at anyone but themselves to blame for their bad grades, politely put your hand over your paper and look the other way. They'll get over it, work harder, drop the class, or flunk out. Their choice is their choice. Your mission is to maximize the investment of your time and tuition to obtain as much knowledge as you can so you can put it to your best use later in life.

Lesson: You are responsible for your outcomes just as others sitting in class with you are responsible for theirs. When in the classroom behave as if your mother or father is standing in the back cheering you on. Now, you know what to do.

How I Studied

Back when I was in grade school and high school, just as it is today, we were assigned homework and tests were scheduled. However, no one taught me effective study techniques and test preparation strategies. Only after my time in the service did things *get real* to the point I actually sat down and thought about it. Yes, people do learn in different ways. For me, the following ideas were very effective.

First, let's talk about where to sit. In almost every college you can sit wherever you like. So where's the best spot? Well, you want to hear and see everything. And you want to limit distraction from the other students. Sometimes the obvious choice is the right one. Sit in the front row center if possible. And if not then as close as you can to it.

Now let's look at it from the professor's perspective. Where do the slackers usually sit? That's right, way in back where they can goof off. Even if you aren't a slacker, you could become guilty by association- thought to be slacker simply by the fact you're hanging out near them. You could also be distracted by slackers or their incessant chatter could rob you of hearing the lectures. I intentionally used the word "rob" because that's what noisy slackers do. If you've either paid your tuition directly or have earned a scholarship through your hard work, slacker behavior can devalue the product you're receiving. So avoid being around them.

Analyzing each professor's approach to tests is important. Some of what you will see on an exam will be from lecture and some from books or assigned reading. While taking notes for each class I wrote the date in the upper right corner of the page and marked the beginning and the ending time of topics covered. After each class I'd bracket sections of notes and write the approximate amount of time per topic. If your professor spends a larger amount of time on a particular topic the likelihood is he thinks it's important and you will see it on an exam. These days you can use free phone apps to record entire lectures; yet another good reason to sit towards the front of the class.

Professors will also use key phrases such as "a word to the wise is sufficient" or the outright obvious "you will see this again" to clue you in that a particular concept will be on a test. Put a big star next to those in your notes.

Some class types such as math and science require the application of formulas to solve problems. In these cases the book or online resources include practice problems. Invest the time to do not only the practice problems but make up your own with slightly different values and do them again and again until the formula and process of solving them simply flows through your mind.

Next, take the most important concepts from your notes and the practice problems and make up your own tests. Don't get caught up in making the perfect test harness or app to feed you test questions. The consumption of time to find *perfect* is just a way to hide from actually practicing. Keep it simple and just put it on paper or a very simple slideshow if needed. Within the controlled confines of the tests you make is a nice, safe box where you can practice controlled failure. Simply take your practice tests again and again until you can ace them. This gets you one step closer to becoming a Curve Breaker. Then, immediately after you take the real in-class test, go back to your notes and highlight which items you just saw and make notes about things on the test that were not in your practice test.

This highlighting and adding a few extra notes serves two purposes:

- These are the items you will see again on a mid-term or final exam.

- They aid in your analysis of how the professor decides what's important to remember.

Professors tend to be pretty consistent in how they test. Some are balanced in putting lecture vs. assigned reading items on tests. Others ignore assigned readings and test almost exclusively on that which they've lectured. Knowing their preferences can help you focus your study time.

Be sure to save your practice tests and the actual ones if you get them back. And if you do, then compare the two and update your practice ones to match. These become great resources to prepare for your mid-term and final.

There were two other things I did to prepare for a test. Where I could I would make up or memorize words. As an example, there's an old one to remember the colors of the rainbow: RoyGBiv. It stands for red, orange, yellow, green, blue, indigo, and violet. You can make up your own words or phrases to help you remember anything. And with respect to math tests, I practiced writing down formulas again and again until I didn't have to look them up. For example, the volume of a sphere can be computed by the formula 4/3 pie * r **3 or four-thirds-pie-r-cubed. That's a simple one, however, one can also remember more complex calculus formulas by writing them again and again and this can help you be more efficient during test taking. At the start of many tests, I started by flipping my paper over and immediately writing down all the formulas or catchy word-phrases I'd practiced. Then during the test I could refer to them as I liked. Using this trick while sitting right in front of the class, right in front of the teacher, he also saw I wasn't cheating.

These days, some professors are also allowing students the use of graphing calculators and testing students online. The techniques I mention are still useful. Adaptation to your situation is the key. And by the way, for readers of this who happen to still be in high school these tactics will work for you right now.

The process of becoming good at something comes through repetition; just doing it again and again. To be the best, the NBA's Stephen Curry practices constantly. And it shows. He and his Golden State Warriors won the basketball championship in 2015. Famed Hollywood actor and musician Will Smith has a great quote on this too, "The separation of talent and skill is one of the greatest misunderstood concepts for people who are trying to excel, who have dreams, who want to do things. Talent you have naturally. Skill is only developed by hours and hours and hours of beating on your craft." Although I didn't directly quote from it, author, Tony Rohn, wrote a nice book on Will Smith and I invite you to find it on Amazon. It's titled: *Will Smith: How To Be Successful In Life - 100 Success Lessons from Will Smith.*

Lesson: Sitting towards the front of the class, organizing your note taking, making and taking practice tests, and analyzing how your professor builds tests can increase the likelihood of you mastering a subject and getting the most value for your dollars and effort. This is a simple decision you need to take.

General Electric Lighting Nela Park Internship

When you look at software job postings, you'll come to notice they usually state they're seeking someone who knows a skill and has some number of years using it. For example, writing code in C# with three years of experience. Reading job posting after posting like this can cause college students without experience much stress. Fear not.

One way to gain some experience has been around for ages and it's perfectly suited to students having only a few months free time in the summers; time between semesters. It's called an *internship*. An internship is an opportunity for an apprentice or student of something to work in a hands-on environment to better his craft. Engineering internships are similar in many ways to trade apprenticeships such as those for carpenters and electricians. However, since virtually every field utilizes technology, internships can vary widely in the type of assignment. My observation has been the pay and professional support one receives during an internship depends upon the laws of supply and demand in the marketplace for the skillset he brings to the table. The easier it is to find someone of your skillset, the less you'll earn and less a company will care whether you stay or go. For example, I've consistently heard that radio station employees are paid nothing and treated quite poorly. Conversely, skills such as software development or analysis are rare and in commercial environments usually offer greater pay and a comfortable environment.

In the spring of my sophomore year at Norfolk State University I blindly applied for several summer internships at larger corporations I considered to be first rate. By blindly I mean these companies weren't advertising for interns, I just mailed them letters requesting to participate out of the blue. Back then there was a really cool book called "Peterson's Guide to Engineering Science and Computer Jobs." This huge reference provided in depth profiles on thousands of corporations and government organizations hiring engineers. These days a simple web search such as "Top software companies in the Inc. 5000" yields similar information. And anyone can run just a few searches to learn about companies and what it's like to live in the cities where they do business.

There were a few things I wanted to accomplish as an intern: gain experience, start to build a good reputation, and earn money to pay for ongoing, non-tuition related expenses such as rent and car maintenance. In applying, I prepared a resume and a nice cover letter in which I stated my appreciation for their specific company, line of business, and interest in becoming part of their team. I also included copies of those letters of recommendation that helped me win the McDaniel Jones academic scholarship and a copy of my letter of commendation from the Commander, U.S. Naval Security Group.

Socioeconomically, I was climbing up from the bottom- a motivated, wanna-be developer if you will. There were no friends who could give me an "in" or hook me up, no buddies of dad who knew someone or connections like that. So I had to build small blocks of trust and then more upon those until I had a measurable track record. That takes persistence, faith, and patience. In America, people really like hard working, humble, polite, positive-team-player, underdogs. So if you are starting from ground zero like I did, I'm telling you it's more than possible to raise yourself up.

One of the companies to which I applied was the headquarters for General Electric Lighting at the National Electric Light Association (NELA) Park in Cleveland, Ohio. One of the reasons I applied to this location was we had family there and I'd have a known, safe place to live. Since I had applied in the blind I really didn't expect a response, so it was a very nice surprise when I opened their letter. G. E. Lighting offered me an internship with pay at the rate of $26,500 per year. Sounds pretty weak, doesn't it?

That was 1987. In 2017 dollars, this equates to an annual rate of roughly $58,008. Not too bad for someone who had just finished his sophomore year of college. It was a very big deal for me as our income that year had been a paltry $9,500. And this opportunity served as a source of inspiration and hope our financial situation would someday improve.

Founded in 1933 and located just seven miles from downtown Cleveland, NELA Park sits upon a beautifully landscaped ninety-two acre college-like campus. It is absolutely gorgeous. The city of Cleveland has evolved over the years from an iron and steel powerhouse to a prime location for innovative health and technology companies. My experience with Cleveland is the people there are authentically friendly and it's a regenerating metropolis. With the Rock & Roll Hall Of Fame, West Side Market, Great Lakes Science Center, Cleveland Aquarium, the Indians, Cavaliers, and Browns, trendy and exotic watering holes such as Edison's and the Velvet Tango Room, and of course American Iron Chef Michael Symons's fantastic restaurant, Lola, I cannot help but agree with comedian Drew Carey there's always something fun to do.

G.E. Lighting at NELA Park was a pretty big operation. At the time, the company had in the neighborhood of fifteen thousand employees at this one location and it seemed to run like a well-oiled machine. There was easy parking, big clean offices, the latest computer equipment, and a lot of energetic and positive-thinking coworkers. My boss, Nick, happened to have been a former Navy man. Remember several paragraphs back where I mentioned building blocks of success that help you later? This was one of those times. My grades were very good, however, having served honorably in the Navy demonstrated my willingness to commit to a team's mission.

Nick, our manager, was a solid businessman with the demeanor of someone who had been in the military a long time. Very organized, confident, and with a buttons-to-zipper gig line that I swear was never askew, he was a polished professional who had roughly a dozen people directly reporting to him. Together we were part of a telecommunications group responsible for the equipment utilized by everyone in the company at this location. Routers, modems, phones, network cables, wiring closets, and more were installed, upgraded, and maintained by this one team. Their responsibilities also included management of local and long distance phone billing for all of NELA Park. While a dozen people might sound like a lot for this, the team had a very deep task list as the fifteen thousand people on campus were organized into scores of departments; each with its own technology needs.

By Tom Nicholas

Upon arrival I was welcomed by the group, given the grand tour of NELA Park, learned some of the extensive history of it, taken to a very nice lunch, and given a cubicle in which to work. The uniform of the day if you will was somewhere between business and business casual. Most members of the team wore dress slacks, short sleeved button down shirt, and a tie. It was professional but a little old school. There were two types of employees from what I observed- those on more of a business track who dressed in a full suit every day and those more on a technical track who openly joked the constrictive nature of a tie would surely cut off the blood circulation to their brains. The ones with ties were either new like me or were seeking to lead teams and run things. The ones without ties were much more interested in research or applied science.

Our team members held a diverse set of skills. There were software developers, network gurus, builders of servers, and some ran cables and built wiring closets. A wiring closet, for the uninitiated, is a small cabinet or room where cable or electrical connections are routed. This was well before wireless connectivity or Wi-Fi. These cabinets were big- just one typically had scores and sometimes hundreds of RJ45 connector wires going into modems and other devices. This part of our team was the not-wearing-a-suit bunch. We applied technology to support various business groups in their efforts to make and sell lighting products. For me it was the perfect place to be. I got to visit many different departments, learned what they did, saw firsthand how they functioned, and gained a bird's eye view of a very important division within a classic American corporation.

My internship assignment was to solve a single problem. Each month the local and long distance telecommunications bills would come in from AT&T on 9-track Centrex tapes. Phone calls, or transactions, were mapped to specific phone numbers. And phone numbers were billed for the particular equipment used at a given location. The monthly bill exceeded five hundred thousand dollars or roughly $1.1 million US in 2017 money. Half of it was long distance billing and half local billing. One of our department's tasks was to read the tapes and parse the billing transactions to the other departments. Any transactions we could not map back to other departments, our department would have to pay out of our own budget. It had reached the point that one quarter of the bill, roughly one hundred twenty five thousand dollars per month was not mapping to other departments and my manager's boss was about to have heart attack.

One of the full time developers was more than happy to hand me a thick, thousand page printout of the source code for the bill mapping program as well as samples for some parts of the monthly bill. He was a larger guy, an Ohio State Buckeye graduate, and had a slight smile on his face as if he were giving zero respect to me; Mr. Noob Guy from little Norfolk State. Eager to make a good impression, I waited till after 6 pm, when most everyone went home, and unfolded the source code half way down a long hallway. Back then software was organized differently. There was no such thing as object-oriented development. No classes, properties, and methods. We had modules, routines, and functions.. *and we liked it!* Actually, no, looking back we just didn't know software could be as elegantly organized as it is today. So with sharp pencil in hand and sprawled out on the floor, I carefully began to bracket off every BEGIN and END block, every FOR and WHILE loop, and more until I could see the different parts and pieces and how they were related.

Creating code and debugging are actually opposite sides of the same coin. If you look at either from ten thousand feet up they can seem very confusing. To be good at either you need to be able to organize confusing parts down into smaller and smaller parts till the bits of logic come together. I'd actually learned this twice and didn't realize it. In the Navy, when I was just twenty-three, my LPO taught me trouble shooting in an area of the NSGD Norfolk, CINCLANTFLT HQ communications center we called Tech Control. This was where the message receiving equipment was and we needed to make sure everything was configured and tuned up just right. And in my freshman computer science classes one of my favorite professors, Dr. C.S. Chu, taught us the same lesson about software design.

Lesson: If a problem looks too big, organize it into smaller and smaller parts until you can solve those parts. Then it will all come into place.

So when my G.E. team member handed me the source code and billing data the challenge felt like no big deal- I knew immediately what I needed to do. It took me one day to block things off and gain a general understanding of how the program functioned. It took another half day to analyze part of a billing record and trace it through for mapping. After several good transactions I bumped into one that wouldn't map. The phone company used unique identifiers called a Universal Service Ordering Codes or USOC codes for short. This transaction had a USOC code mapped to a phone number, however, the code was unknown. In the non-mapped case our department would just eat the cost- because we couldn't prove it belonged to another department.

Turned out there were lots and lots of unmapped USOC codes. Boom. Done. It was that simple. The next morning I asked for a meeting with my boss, Nick, and the software developer who handed me the code. I suggested we obtain the latest USOC code list from AT&T and update our program. With big smiles on their faces they agreed. But then it got a little awkward. Nick said, "Well, that was your assignment for this entire summer internship and you solved it in a day and a half. We need to come up something more for you to do."

For the next two weeks I worked with the wiring closet technicians. We went from closet to closet, upgrading modems and figuring out why some lines were working and some weren't. It was then I realized why wiring closets need locks. When left unlocked virtually anyone can reroute anything and some cases they did. One closet in particular had over two hundred connections, none of the lines were tagged or numbered, and it looked like a total rats nest. Box by box, line by line, connection by connection we replaced and tagged everything. It was very tedious work but important to the mission of supporting the business. However, it also served as inspiration that more interesting work was on the horizon if I were to stay in school and finish my degree.

Once the USOC codes were updated in the billing software, Nick and his boss were very happy; for about a week. Billing ran, transactions mapped, and departments notified. That week was the amount of time it took before the downstream department managers had heart attacks of their own. Over the many months of increasingly unmapped USOC codes they had seen their phone billing dwindle significantly. Once we updated the software they got whacked with their true bills. As you will come to learn once you get into the field, when business people don't like what they are seeing, engineers have to defend their code and their procedures for creating it. With no more evidence than a dramatically higher bill, our department was accused of having new bugs in our software. So we then formally confirmed our quality assurance process and stood firm.

The next step in making things better for G.E. at NELA Park was analysis of each department's bill. One by one they were coming to us and emphatically stating "This equipment isn't ours. Why are we being billed for it?"

To help them, we took their bills and traced back each phone number to a line in a particular office. NELA Park was big- huge in fact. With so many departments and so many offices it's understandable that over time things got lost in the shuffle. People moved. Departments moved. Spaces were converted. And so it was. In department after department we discovered people had moved from one location to another; setting up a new phone system in the new office but not disconnecting the old one. We still had to pay for old, active connections even if they weren't being utilized. Likewise for converted spaces. We found entire office spaces had been converted to storage rooms complete with dozens of paid phone and network connections no one was using. One by one these were addressed, disconnected, and removed from future billing. And when all was said and done there was an updated company protocol for relocating and reapportioning space. And this too you will see in your career. Identifying the *root cause* for an issue is important. Equally valuable is helping your organization come up with a plan to prevent bad things from happening in the future.

In the final four weeks of my G.E. internship I was asked to help complete a task from my boss Nick's to-do list. He had been evaluating telecommunications management software packages in the one hundred thousand dollar price range and wanted a more in depth analysis. They had reached out to several vendors and the sales teams of those software companies viewed G.E. Lighting as the big whale of contracts- one about which they could brag and from which they'd make great ongoing support and licensing revenue. My role was two-fold: conduct research and keep the sales people off Nick's radar till the company was ready for more formal conversations. *It was in this role where my character and ethics were to be tested.*

Sales teams for large companies oftentimes have nice, big marketing budgets. Legally they deduct from pre-tax profits: airline tickets, car rentals, hotel stays, small gifts, as well as meals and entertainment. Entertainment expenses that are both ordinary and necessary in carrying on a trade or business are deductible when they meet the criteria in United States Internal Revenue Service publication 463. And companies are by no means bashful in lavishing them on prospective clients. It's considered an investment towards longer term profit.

Our team had done a cursory or minimal overview of a few telecommunications management software packages, however, we needed more in depth information and we needed to consider offerings from more vendors. So, with a list they had provided in hand, I picked up the phone and started making calls. The typical sales process starts with the vendor attempting to qualify and quantify the value of a prospect to their business. Vendors try to figure out whether your company is a *guppy*, one that won't generate much revenue, or a *whale*- one that would. Once I identified us as G.E. Lighting and stated our phone bill was half a million dollars a month it seemed I'd suddenly made new friends for life. Information deluged in, I got to see live demos, and with each presentation they provided I was able to come up with a better list of questions for the next. The responses to these would provide the meat of my analysis and final report. Then to get a better idea of their pricing flexibility I mentioned to teach I was evaluating the packages of their competitors. That's when it got interesting.

These sales teams wanted to influence my decision; our decision. They wanted contact information for my boss, Nick, and his boss as they realized a twenty-five year old wasn't going to make a one hundred thousand dollar decision alone. But I was under strict orders not to divulge this information and stuck to my guns- telling them I was there to analyze their offering. Unable to gain direct access to our management team they then decided to try to influence my report. They offered to take me downtown to some of the nice restaurants and clubs, to Cleveland Indian baseball games, concerts, and more. They described this as a chance to get to know us better, however, from an ethical perspective let me tell you now this is a very slippery slope.

While awaiting my top secret clearance from the U.S. Navy we were lectured on what it took to remain uncompromised and in good standing. One of the biggest things is one cannot open himself up to blackmail. You see, once you start taking favors from a vendor it can be used against you in conversation, correspondence, or in worse case scenarios being tagged in social media- where your company can see it.

Whether you're a politician taking hundreds of thousands of dollars in campaign contributions or point person in evaluating expensive software packages, people you barely know don't give you money or valuable things without there being the expectation of quid pro quo. You give them something, they give you something- like that. The problem with this kind of arrangement is it jeopardizes your objectivity, puts your organization at risk due to a potentially bad decision, weighs on your conscience because you know it's morally wrong, and in the end can ruin your personal reputation. Flat out, it can make you miserable and get you fired. So don't take such favors or gifts.

Lesson: For your opinions and reputation to remain pure they must be free from improper influence. Living this way demonstrates character and integrity and garners the genuine respect of your peers.

Over those weeks I was able to recognize these temptations, resist them, and generate a comprehensive fifty plus page report comparing and contrasting several software packages and narrowing them down to two very good ones. During the last few days I was also invited to several meetings, one of which was the damnedest things I'd ever seen.

Remember a several paragraphs back when I mentioned there were generally two types of professionals I'd met at G.E. Lighting- the business type and the applied science type? In one of my last big meetings I met the man who could surely been in consideration for G.E. Lighting's King of Software Geeks.

As the story goes, we entered a larger, well appointed, perfectly square conference room full of department heads wearing fancy three piece suits and fancy Italian business shoes. They were sitting in the nicer chairs, each with what could be described as a footman, acolyte or for lack of a better term minion. The team member who brought me to the meeting had obviously been to these before, pointed to the chairs against the back wall, and whispered, "Sit here quietly and watch this." The meeting was scheduled for 10 AM. At 10:02 the looks on the faces of the executives at the big meeting table began to sour. By 10:06 the men in suits began to fidget. By 10:10 they were openly discussing sending a hunting expedition for the presenter.

Sporting classic Ray Ban sunglasses atop his head, a smooth looking polo shirt, khaki shorts, and wearing flip-flops he entered the room and immediately apologized for being late. "Traffic," was all he said, shaking his head back and forth. Too busy to lecture him on it the department heads simply nodded in understanding. He brought no notes, had no binders, no books; just himself. And he didn't take a seat. Standing at the head of the room he confidently asked, "Gentlemen, we are ready for the upgrade to of the VAX mainframe operating system. I've published a schedule that does much of the work off hours to minimize impacts to our business. Let's walk through it. Feel free to ask questions along the way."

For the next forty five minutes he adeptly answered every single question without hesitation. Technical questions related to operational impacts, scheduling questions related to production, and more. He knew his material inside and out and the exact needs of every client he supported. Yes, even computer scientists have clients. In fact, every person he served and those you will someday serve, *are clients.* By meting's end the businessmen were completely satisfied and the operating system upgrade plan locked in.

He then thanked them for their time and walked out. I told my office mate I wanted to meet him so we tried to catch up. But he was too quick. We made it out to the parking lot but he was zipping off, sunglasses on, in his speedy corvette; never to be seen by me again.

"Who is that guy?" I asked. My buddy told me he had been with the company for several years, was their operating systems expert, and had an unusual arrangement. For six months of the year he worked twelve hours a day, six days a week. The company had positioned a mini-computer in his home so he could do support work from there as well. The other six months he was off and rumor was he was pursuing his doctorate degree.

If your vision of the perfect position is that one, let me tell you jobs like that do exist. But there is a tradeoff for having that one- lack of human interaction. There are many types of computer scientists, software engineers, and developers. Some have a lot of human contact and some have less. The big challenge with positions having less human contact is in the full development of one's people skills. You remember how socially backward the character "Sheldon" was from TV's "The Big Bang Theory"? Although *smart is the new sexy*, most people who met Sheldon eventually wanted to beat him with a stick because of his lack of people skills.

Our G.E. Lighting operating system expert had worked his way into the position *and* honed his people skills along the way. That meeting opened my eyes to the idea software engineers could play many roles in the real world. I imagine him in the corvette still zipping along Route 283 and the beautiful view of Lake Erie. And good on him!

As for the summer internship with G.E. Lighting, my work was completed and that was that. Over my summer stay in Ohio, I was living with an aunt and uncle in their 70's. My uncle was an expert carpenter who had a very nice career with U.S. Steel. They enjoyed the typical suburban life where he worked and she raised the kids. However, through the years they had also endured World War II, the Korean War, Vietnam, presidential assassination, and lots of political and economic turmoil. These experiences had colored their perception, especially my aunt's perception, of the world, the country, and of hope for a positive future. In my last week with them we started discussing next steps. What would happen after graduation? Would we take a position with G.E. and come live nearby in Ohio? And what, financially, would be an acceptable offer?

I told them G.E. Lighting was amazing. Their business was strong, dynamic, and evolving. They offered great pay, opportunity for advancement, and encouraged engineers to continue furthering their education. And to a person, everyone I met at G. E. Lighting was nice. So what would be an acceptable offer?

$30,000 per year, no less. That's the amount I suggested was my minimum upon graduation in two years. In 2017 dollars that's around $65,669. My aunt, stuck in the mindset of the 1950's and 1960's thought me unrealistic, and without openly saying it, almost greedy. Now one can look at money two ways- from a perspective of selfishness and greed or from one of pay for performance. Once again companies generally pay based upon the laws of supply and demand. If your skillset is easy to obtain, say you sweep floors, they don't have to pay a lot for you because they could find someone else to do it in two seconds. However, if your skillset is rare and in demand, such as software engineering, the marketplace commands they pay you more.

To very loosely paraphrase actor Will Smith in the movie, "Hitch," [Once they've hired you] they've already agreed to go out with you. Your job is to simply not mess it up. If you earn the opportunity to participate in an internship, make the most of it. My time at G.E. Lighting was a meaningful, valuable, and special period in my life. Whether you are looking for a longer term place to build a career or simply an opportunity to learn before branching out on your own, I invite you to consider investing time with General Electric. It is one of America's big time corporations, a great place for new engineers to build a solid reputation, and they definitely know what they are doing.

Lesson: After college, a great place to bridge the gap between your formal engineering education and the hard-nosed, fast paced business world is a profitable, large corporation. Unlike start-ups struggling to survive, larger companies do their best to invest in educating their employees in formal quality processes required to create solid products. That knowledge proves valuable as you advance in your career.

The Lost Boys

It can happen anytime and at almost any point in one's life- the distraction that takes a person so off course from the pursuit of a dream that a great opportunity becomes lost. I've seen young men and women get distracted in high school over each other, which is almost a rite of passage, and I've seen something even worse in college.

Back in the late 1980's computer gaming was just getting going. Early graphical versions of role playing games similar to World Of Warcraft were just coming online and although crude in design they were equally addictive. In the Norfolk State University library, then on the first floor, were a hundred or so computer terminals;

available for anyone's use. Someone had installed one of these games on them and it was beginning to sap the time from students. Initially, I saw one or two kids playing one but I ignored it as earlier in my life I'd become immune to the distraction. As a teenager I squandered hundreds of dollars in quarters I'd earned playing classic arcade games with my friends. I saw what little money I'd earned literally disappear.

When these kinds of games became free on the network, the loss of money became a non-factor. The hidden poison was the loss of time. There is only so much of it you get in life and even less of it is freely-available while in school. My parents weren't paying for my school and if I was going to eat I had to focus on studying during the day and getting my butt to work at 7-11 nights.

Not so for some of my classmates. One of them in particular started playing the game more and more. And it started to reflect in his grades. Eventually he started missing classes and afterwards I'd pop over to the library only to find him parked in the same spot. I'd say, "Dude, you totally blew off Dr. So-and-So's class. What's up?" Like a crack addict, he'd tell me he got caught up leveling and then simply mumble something incoherent. His parents were providing his tuition, room, board, car payment, gas, food, and walking around money- an amazing opportunity to become anything he wanted had been literally laid at his feet. Eventually he stopped going to class altogether and apparently his mom and pop didn't like grades that go "D," "D," "F," "F," "F." And the next semester, he was gone. Done. And never to be seen again.

He had a free ride and had made it through Calculus I & II but completely blew it due to a video game.

Now am I writing you should give up video games altogether? Nope, not at all. In fact you're reading the book written by someone who, with my friends Ben, Mike, Vince, Joe, and Dave leveled a Troll Hunter named "Bonestank" to Level 85 in World of Warcraft before shifting to World Of Tanks under the same user name. So what's the difference between me and the Lost Boy? *Time management.*

One of the things that benefited me the most was learning to identify the important things in my life and prioritize them.

- Family responsibilities: Helping out around the house, cleaning the kitchen, taking out the trash, doing my laundry, investing time simply talking with my parents and siblings. Why is this first? Because, of virtues, love is the greatest and these are specific ways you can demonstrate it at home.

- Exercise and sleep: Taking care of my body by breaking a good hard sweat and eating right is essential to good health. If there's a TV commercial for what I was about to put in my mouth, I tried not to eat very much of it. Marinate on that one for a minute.

- Homework, spiritual, and intellectual growth: Identify what is due, how long it's going to take, and the priority or timing of it needing to be done. After homework, I chose some things I found interesting and added them into the mix. For me the extra things were ancient philosophy, robotics, and fishing. You get the idea.

- Playtime: I also enjoyed computer gaming. Back then my favorite was an Electronic Arts (EA) game called, "The Seven Cities Of Gold." In it you'd negotiate with the King or Queen of a European country for a ship, crew, and supplies and then sail across to North, South, or Central America to explore and establish colonies. It was great fun and didn't require coins to play each time.

For each of the categories above I mapped out the time I had in a given day and prioritized what I was going to do. When you are on a trek to accomplish something great you must be organized. For me gaming was an important way to relax, however, I rewarded myself with time for it after having completed the other items in the list.

One of my favorite American historical figures is Dr. Benjamin Franklin. An accomplished diplomat, inventor, and founding father of the United States he is quoted as having said, "Moderation in everything- including moderation." How could this statement be interpreted and adapted to your benefit? Having a plan and a schedule is critical to your success, however, life is also meant to be enjoyed. As long as you're caught up and on track with your goals, it can be great fun to throw caution to the wind and really enjoy life.

For me that has sometimes taken the form of going white water rafting, dancing with friends till 3 AM, and yes, even enjoying a Geek Fest with Ben, Mike, Jim, Vince, Joe, and Dave where we online game for a solid 12 hours on a Saturday. But those are rare treats I give myself for having worked hard toward my academic goals.

Lesson: Personal success requires you live a purpose-filled life where you focus on your focus and control the type and time allotted to life's distractions. Your plan mapped to a timeline is your roadmap to success. Find a quiet place and make one. Be a little open to adjusting but only due to circumstances beyond your control. Then with great optimism and shameless fervor chase your dream.

Benefits Of College Clubs & Associations

Engineers have been stereotyped as having big gaps when it comes to the social graces. In the movie, "The Social Network," even techno-phenom Mark Zuckerberg is portrayed as having had what we call interface agreement challenges. Successful human interactions, like properly communicating APIs, are strongly-typed but loosely-coupled. "Well what the heck does that mean?" you might ask. Good question.

In the case, say, of two friends each is an individual person with parts of this life unique to him; parts that don't intersect. This is the loosely coupled part. However, there are also parts of their lives that do intersect. These parts help define their relationship. These are the strongly-typed parts. Let's define them in terms of object oriented design or OOD. In OOD we define an object as having properties and methods.

Relationship properties, hypothetically, could include that you and I both enjoy solving triple integration by parts with trig substitutions equations, Maroon 5 music, sleeping in on Saturdays, our burgers well-done with BBQ sauce, non-obfuscated code, brunettes with big brown eyes, playing World Of Tanks, and The Big Bang Theory TV show.

Our strongly-typed methods, alternatively, could include parameters of me only calling you after 10 AM Saturday morning, cooking your burger properly when I host, and gracefully pulling you into the conversation I'm having with a new hottie brunette with big brown eyes.

So how do we get from New Geeksburg, where we live now, to this utopian happy-place? Well it's better described as a journey than a destination. There are full sections in bookstores about how to win friends and influence people and even a fantastic book with that exact title. In a nutshell, it comes down to being interested in other people and the wonders of life going on around you. It's becoming the anti-Sheldon if you will. Sure, Sheldon Cooper of The Big Bang Theory had interests, however, the way they were explored in the first few seasons of the TV character's life were oftentimes very selfish, rude, and off-putting.

Consider, your appreciation for a given topic, hobby, or even event can be enhanced by interacting with others having the same interest and investing intellectually in their perspective. Think to yourself whether or not their ideas on something make sense for you too. They may, they may not. Either way, they open your mind to new possibilities and the experiences can be a fun way to make new friends. Invite others to talk and then simply, appreciatively, listen.

Every college and university has an almost never-ending stream of fun and interesting activities, events, and clubs to help students blend in and become part of the social fabric of the place. While attending Norfolk State University I noticed lots and lots of things to do. With my limited time I needed to be selective of course but after football I still wanted to find something interesting; something more-related to my major. And sure enough, one of my favorite computer science professors, Dr. Sandra DeLoatch, made an announcement in-class about The Association For Computing Machinery or ACM. At the time of this writing and as described on their website, the ACM is the world's largest educational and scientific computing society, delivering resources that advance computing as a science and a profession. They have Special Interest Groups (SIGs), a wide variety of scientific publications, educational activities, a learning center, career & job center, and much more. It's definitely something worth checking out.

In my sophomore year I joined our local chapter. We had distinguished speakers talk with us about computing history, how the science is evolving and could affect the future of the world, opportunities we could pursue paths for getting there, and more. My advisor, Dr. George Harrison demonstrated a very cool mathematical proof, we participated in Norfolk State's homecoming with an admittedly geekish NSU spirit float, and enjoyed a cool offsite Halloween Party. All in all it was lots of fun and I made many new friends as we primarily focused around our shared interest: computer science.

Being an active member in such clubs can also offer opportunities to develop your leadership skills. In my junior year I became the student chapter President of the organization, led meetings, organized bake sales and activities and was privileged to introduce our special speakers; including Dr. DeLoatch.

In preparing for her introduction I watched videos on how professionals did it. These days you can find similar ones on YouTube. I met with her to chat about her topic of discussion, her experiences at the University of Michigan and William & Mary, and how she came to be head of our then Math & Computer Science Department. The goal of an introduction is to ready the audience for the wisdom about to be imparted upon them and open their eyes to the credibility the speaker brings. This was my first opportunity as the ACM chapter President to introduce anyone, let alone someone of her stature, and I wanted to get it just right. Her advice was invaluable and the event was perfectly done. From there our year was smooth sailing and proved enlightening and fun.

One of the things I came to realize on a small scale while being part of our ACM is computer science people, nay technology people, are part of a really big community. When we are in school and taking classes we don't really get that "we're one big team" feeling. I now think this because as students haven't yet "made the team." We haven't proven our ability to understand complex concepts and we haven't utilized them in real world situations. No disrespect intended to aspiring technology professionals, in fact deep down we want for you to become amazing, successful, engineers who help us advance science and make the world better. But first, you need the formal education. It's the foundation upon which everything else is built. And joining organizations like the ACM can open your eyes to a bright big world!

Lesson: From the moment you exit the doors of the university and take that first position you'll be on a team where the sharing of ideas is not only helpful, it's essential to its success and survival. College clubs and associations help you hone your people skills while having fun and can make you a better teammate later. Join in, it's fun!

Professors As Favorite Aunts & Uncles

Growing up, I was the oldest of four children and all my siblings were sisters. I had no older brother to give me advice and no younger brother to whom I could give it. And my dad willingly sacrificed working ungodly overtime hours to keep a roof over our heads, clothes on us, and food on the table so I missed seeing him as much as I would have liked. I guess you could say there was a bit of an older-male void in my life. So it wasn't until I was in the U.S. Navy that I began to appreciate that kind non-parental mentoring. And college is very different than high school when it comes to that as well.

In college I came to learn professors can be mentors as well as educators. That is, they see your mind opening and when you show sincere interest in their topics a symbiotic relationship can begin to blossom. On the one hand they see your eyes open wide in understanding and potentially extending concepts about which they are passionate and have invested intellectual energy. You are really "getting" their topic. On the other hand, your insights and fresh perspective have the possibility to help them think in totally new ways. Just because they're teaching doesn't mean they're done growing. Most professors I've known remain active in their field. They conduct meaningful research, publish papers, and speak in front of their peers.

Your professors aren't your parents but they also aren't your peers. So I prefer to consider them favorite aunts and uncles. In non-class times, they have office hours; times when you can meet and talk with them about your class, your major, what it's like to teach at a the college level, and what it's like out in the real world. My mentors if you will included: Dr. Harrison (academic advisor), Dr. DeLoatch (department head), Dr. Chu (our cross between Yoda and Sun Tzu), Dr. Smithy (literature), Dr. Brown (world civilization), and football coach Mr. Tom Morris. In their own way, each of them imparted nuggets of wisdom I use even to this day.

And so I really encourage you to get to know your professors as they have insights you'll find no place else.

Which Language Should You Learn First?

The which-programming-language-first question may well be the most asked by people interested in the software field today. Even I didn't know which to choose. Thankfully, my college guided us in a particular direction. The whole of computing space is still expanding from its own version of The Big Bang. That is, arguably, the advent of the personal computer in the late 1970's was the catalyst that flung the world forward on a trajectory of ever expanding of technological achievement.

Prior to the 1980's most use of computers was limited to big businesses and large entities with deep pockets to afford them such as governments and their agencies. The creation of smaller hardware and the operating systems to go with them led to further development of programming languages. This is all stuff taught in common Introduction To Computer Science courses- so I'll skip ahead.

Technology creation and software development go through cycles. Hardware companies come out with cool new gadgets and then software companies and independent developers maximize gadget potential; oftentimes bringing hardware to its processing knees so to speak. And then hardware companies come out with the next big thing and the cycle repeats. If you were to ask the which-language-to-learn question at any point over the past thirty years, you'd likely get a different set of top five answers each time. So where does that leave you?

Let me offer three short points to shed some light.

- Almost every language supports a common set of elements.

    Input: It reserves words for getting data into the computing device; for example through keyboard, file, http stream, or a microphone.

    Output: It reserves words for pushing data out of the device; for example visual display, audio, print outs, files, and more.

    Math: Commands exist for making arithmetic calculations on data. And in reality everything is converted into numbers- even string comparisons. Determining whether "mypassword" is the same as "notmypassword" is done mathematically. The letters are represented in the computer as ASCII character codes or numbers and those numbers are what are actually compared.

    Conditional Evaluation: The language reserves words to test whether a condition is true or false. For example, "If (x==y) then { do some other code things };"

    Looping: The language provides some combination of words or symbols to allow a collection of instructions to be executed over and over until some condition is met.

    All languages have this minimum set of elements and this hasn't changed over the decades. What has changed is the tools that help us organize our work. These tools make code easier to read, maintain, and reuse, and the operating systems that continue to grow and support more complex commands.

    So, the likelihood is good you'll want to choose a newer language or a newer version of an existing language because technology and the market supports it. For example, Java and C# would both beat out Fortran 77 today.

- Online I found a pretty cool article written by Quincy Larson of Free Code Camp. It's titled, "Which programming language should you learn first?"

Quincy has some well-informed opinions but one of the things I really enjoyed is his sprawling flow chart that guides people through the decision making process. Google and the article comes right up- it's worth the read.

- The last point to consider when choosing is to ask, "What in your mind helps make the world a good, nice, hopeful place?" Come up with a short list of companies that do these things in places you'd like to live. Then search the job sites for positions in those companies. Read the languages mentioned in those job descriptions. And there you go.

The first language you learn well will be much like your first childhood friend. You'll remember it forever. However, in your lifetime you'll come to know likely a dozen more just as closely and each of them will have a special place too. At any given time, you'll be great at just the current one and this is normal. So just choose one, learn it well, and keep moving forward.

Adapt & Overcome

Throughout your career as an engineer, you are going to be presented with business and technical puzzles that will require very creative, even unorthodox solutions. Sometimes the problems themselves are messy and sometimes there will be time constraints making more traditional approaches impossible. In my junior year of college I bumped into a tough one and had to get creative. It was the course called Assembly Language II and the assignment was to build a fully functional word processor using assembler; in under two weeks.

During that time I had a number of other assignments also due and wish as we might our professors didn't collaborate on due dates. Sometimes I just got slammed and this was one of those times. For a few hours I sat down and outlined the functionality needed for building a word processor. That was easy enough. However, rather quickly it became clear there wasn't enough time to build in all the functionality required and meet the deadline. Assembly language is very low level stuff. Imagine trying to build a camping shelter with toothpicks. Working in assembly language is like that, all.. the.. time.

In our course, the venerable Dr. Shah had introduced us to the program called MASM. This app read our Assembly language source code and converted it into an executable we could run. He also told us about, but didn't show us, another program called a "disassembler." Disassemblers go the other way- taking an executable program (.exe file) and converting it into Assembly language. We didn't get too much into discussing the use of the disassembler, only that one could reverse engineer applications with it.

At home I had recently purchased a PC and a few programs, including one of the earlier software development environments called, "Turbo Pascal." Pascal was an earlier language often taught in introductory college courses. Back then, it was the first one we learned at Norfolk State. You can see where this is going right?

I was good at Pascal; very good. So at home I took the word processor project outline I had created and built one awesome, fully functional word processor in Turbo Pascal. Next I ran the executable of it against the disassembler and voila- an Assembly language word processor file.

The code it generated was gigantic yet flawless. I used the MASM program to run it and prove the disassembly/reassembly process worked. Then I loaded the disassembled program file into Microsoft's Notepad and edited it to add comments and rename variables to things more meaningful for traceability. Then I saved it MASM'd and tested it again. Boom. Done.

If I had tried to write the word processor by hand I would likely have not finished and the likelihood was high it wouldn't have worked properly due to all the manual hexadecimal offset memory address calculations required to jump from one area of code to another. Briefly I thought using the disassembler/assembler Turbo Pascal approach might have been academically-improper but then I thought about it. Academically-improper would have been working with another student or copying from another student. I did neither of those things. I pulled together pieces of technology the professor told us about and leveraged them.

The greater goal of the assignment was not to see us struggle and go down in flames, not to live Star Trek's no-win scenario of the Kobayashi Maru, but to demonstrate our creativity in building an effective solution. It received an "A" grade.

Lesson: Before diving head-long into a project, consider that most problems have more than one solution. Weigh the pros and cons before choosing a particular path. Often you'll save yourself time and even come up with solutions more elegant than you had initially imagined.

Don't Mess With King Kung

In an earlier chapter I discussed the idea people only mess or play with you if they like you. Although this is true, when you are the one doing the playing it's important to know your audience. One of the more challenging, required technology classes at Norfolk State University is Operating Systems. At the time, this junior level course was taught by Professor Emeritus of Computer Science, Dr. Mou-Liang Kung.

Surviving this class had become a rite of passage for students and it had become the Computer Science equivalent of Calculus II in mathematics. We'd heard stories of students flaming out on this one course and that reputation for academic challenge had, in our small circle, caused us to give the professor the nickname King Kung. For the most part Dr. Kung looked and was all business. However, every now and then we'd get a laugh or smile out of him and he was an approachable man. About a week before mid-terms I was feeling really good about myself, my prospects for earning an "A" grade in his class, and took things just a little bit too far.

That semester I was working in one of the computer labs utilized by all university students. I'd be there to make sure students were connecting properly, understood how to use the computers, and offer helpful advice should they get stuck using Microsoft Access, Excel, and similar programs. Fifty percent of the time things were quiet and students cruised through their work. During one of those quiet times a buddy and I noticed Dr. Kung off to one side, intently working and typing to get something done. Turned out he was doing research for a project and writing a paper.

In one of our previous class periods with him we'd discussed computer security, the importance of protecting your computing environment, and what can happen when one doesn't do that. Throughout life I've been the kind of fun-loving, mischievous imp whose friends at some point shake their collective heads and say, "That's just Tom." Oftentimes it turns out to be great fun for everyone. *This wasn't to be one of those times.*

Back then PCs used DOS as their operating system. This was a little before Microsoft Windows. You'd boot up the computer, the operating system would load, and then you could run programs from there. The joke with which I came up was to write a small app that would also load at boot time and mimic the operating system. It looked and behaved exactly like DOS. However, when you typed in a command it would choose a random error to throw, deny you access to the machine, and redisplay the command prompt. It could easily be terminated with the right keystroke but if you didn't know that you appeared to be stuck. A good LOL for you and me but to the Professor Emeritus of Computer Science, not so much.

My buddy and I perched in our wheeled corner office chairs to watch the show. The professor tried, looked befuddled, tried again, and got frustrated. We stated to laugh, a little at first, then too much. He got quiet, looked, and then summoned us over. Immediately I confessed to what I'd done. Turned out he was working on a very important research paper and the disk he was using had his paper and his data and my joke made him think it had been wiped out. Although relieved, he was less than amused and said to me, "Oh you're a funny guy? You seem to have a lot of free time on your hands. Perhaps you should be studying harder?"

Realizing I'd pole vaulted over the line-of-acceptability I immediately apologized and vowed never to do it again. And off we went. Life was good or so I thought. In the coming weeks I noticed Dr. Kung's interest in my mastering his class seemed more pointed. He wanted to make sure I thoroughly understood each concept. In pirate lingo, there was no quarter given and no shelter or protection to receive partial credit for mostly correct answers. And I brought this all on myself. In the end I worked as hard as I could and was grateful to have earned a "B" grade in Dr. Kung's Operating Systems course.

Lesson: A little fun now and then is a healthy thing but what goes around comes around. And if you don't know your audience it could come back on you big time. So tread carefully.

Alpha Kappa Mu Academic Honor Society

Clubs, organizations, fraternities, and sororities are everywhere on college campuses and there are always students talking about fun things to do. Conspicuous by the absence of chatter about them, membership in an academic societies are also a way to enjoy comradery among your peers and make new friends. Additionally, these organizations further inspire students to become their best.

When I walked off the Norfolk State University football field for the last time, I felt a very big void in my heart. I knew I was never going to play college sports again. A typical male in my twenties, I was trying to take that leap of faith after having read Napoleon Hill's "Think And Grow Rich" book chapter on the mystery of transmuting or converting virtually limitless energy to more useful purposes. Put more simply, I couldn't whack people on the football field so I was looking for more academically-oriented pursuits.

When you work your life-plan and stick to it good things can happen. Good grades lead to all kinds of opportunities that won't otherwise present themselves.

For me, in my junior year, things really began to come together. One day I received a letter in the mail inviting me to become a part of the Alpha Kappa Mu Academic Honor society.

AKM was founded at Tennessee A & I College (now known as Tennessee State University) in Nashville, Tennessee in 1937. To qualify for admission, a student must be registered as full time, in good standing with the institution at which the chapter is located, be at least a junior in a degree program, have completed fifty percent of the requirements for graduation, have a minimum grade-point average of 3.3, where A = 4.0, be ranked in the upper ten percent of the class, exemplify good character, and exhibit the potential for leadership and service.

Chapter meetings on our campus proved to be a great opportunity to meet and get to know other top-flight students. Members were vibrant with energy about their chosen fields, happy to share information on most any topic, and very friendly. Don't worry though about finding them. If your grades are good, their leadership team will find you.

Lesson: Schools and national organizations love to recognize academic excellence. You know who else loves to recognize it? You guessed it, graduate schools and employers. Earned memberships in academic socities are noticed on resumes. Many people are successful without super high GPAs but good grades lead to opportunities that can help you take a straighter path to building your happy future.

Bell Communications Research Internship, Piscataway, New Jersey

One of the beautiful things about pursuing a college major needed in the marketplace is corporations look for you. And when you realize you are in the driver's seat as an engineer, you then owe it to yourself to choose a company that is a good fit. Over the Christmas holiday of my junior year I again turned to Peterson's Guide to Engineering Science and Computer Jobs to look for a good summer internship opportunity. General Electric Lighting was a wonderful experience, however, I wanted to balance out my resume and see what else was out there. Being originally from New Jersey, that's where I set my sights. Centrally located between the major cities of Philadelphia and New York, New Jersey is full of opportunity; especially in the areas of biopharmaceuticals, technology, and transportation.

While a number of good companies were listed, the two that immediately stood out were Bell Labs and Bell Communications Research. Way back in 1879 Alexander

Graham Bell, inventor of the telephone, created the Bell Telephone Company. This company maintained a monopoly on U.S. telephone service until the government split it up in 1982. Out of that eventually sprung AT&T with its R&D team at Bell Labs. The other part were the so-called Baby Bells; Ameritech, Bell Atlantic, Bell South, NYNEX, Pacific Telesis, Southwestern Bell, and US West. The baby bells also had an R&D arm known as Bell Communications Research or Bellcore. And that's where I set my sights.

Reaching out to Bellcore with a simple phone call I was able to obtain their summer internship application. Fingers crossed I waited and waited and then it came. Success! Truth be told I also applied to several other companies but for the sake of brevity and the fact that's where I went, I'll tell this story. Being accepted for a summer internship at Bellcore in 1989 was a really big deal. Each year over 3,000 prospective engineers applied from the best schools in the nation. Of those, only 300 were accepted.

Bellcore was located in Piscataway, New Jersey, just a short distance from the campus of Rutgers University. The company and the university had an arrangement to house summer interns and free bussing back and forth was included. In addition we were paid a percentage of our eventual full salary; roughly $28,500 per year. The best thing about working for any organization shouldn't be the money and benefits but for the sake of argument I'll lay out what was explained at that time.

Bellcore's entry plan was that engineers having just received their bachelor's degree would participate in a specially-designed, one year master's degree program available through a select list of prestigious universities. These included all the Ivy League schools plus M.I.T., Stanford, Caltech, the University Of Michigan, and one or two others. The plan of study was a hybrid of computer science and business. During the year, Bellcore would pay all tuition, books and fees, and pay the engineer roughly half his starting salary. Upon graduation from the program the freshly-minted engineer would come to work for Bellcore and start with a salary of $50,000. In 2017 dollars this is about $109,449. These are rough numbers but reasonably close and very impressive for people with an education but no real experience.

Upon arrival to the Rutgers campus we were welcomed, walked through an indoctrination of sorts, met our preassigned roommates, and invited to a get acquainted party that night. The event was a mixer of sorts and the plan for the summer was laid out. In a way it felt surreal, engineers and Bellcore employees engaging in a kind of supercharged cheer-fest. It was unlike anything I'd seen before and I didn't quite know how to process it. Work nights for me at the 7-11 were long, tedious, and I promise you absolutely nobody cheered when we put out the new microwaveable burritos. Still in all, I liked what Bellcore was doing as it was very warm and welcoming.

At Bellcore the entire summer was carefully planned. When it came to business- they were all business. However, they weren't shy about showing their playful side either. I was assigned to work in an office with two employees as different as different could be. Like General Electric, Bellcore had two distinct tracks; one for employees more interested in business and one for those inclined towards research and development. My businessman office mate came to work every day looking spiffy, wearing a three piece suit and shoes so shiny I almost had to squint when looking at them. My other office mate, Mr. R&D, was the exact opposite. He was serious when it came to science but when it came to office attire his uniform of the day was shorts, flip flops, and a Batman tee shirt. Again, I didn't know how to mentally process this environment.

The Bellcore internship assignment was purely scientific and felt like Jedi training. They had invented a programming language called "L.0." This was a language designed for the specification and simulation of protocols that assumed a true concurrency model. It was well suited for specification of the hierarchical message structure often assumed in telecommunications protocols. So what does all this mean?

L.0 made it easier to design and build solutions to process messaging queue items (packets of data) in parallel. When a message is sent from one place to another, across the internet for example, it doesn't go as one big message. It's segmented into data packets and the route or server connections packets take from Point A to Point Z can vary widely- meaning multiple intermediate servers could be involved in relaying them based on internet traffic and other factors. The high level goal is to reassemble or serialize the message on the other end back into its original form. Consider an L.0 application to be the pump pushing the water through the Slip-n-Slide that carries your message. Across America I'm sure scientists are cringing and wishing they could thwack me in my kneecaps with a wiffle ball bat but in laymen's terms, that's a reasonable description.

There was a team of engineers working this overall development and they did a really nice job describing the project's goal, the language, and my particular role. We had twice a week meetings with our project manager and I was occasionally invited to sit in on other department's meetings just to get a feel for parts of the company.

For the first seven weeks we were making great progress but then a life event happened for me that superseded the internship.

On Friday, June 23rd at 11:20 PM my beautiful daughter, Christina was born. Weighing in at only 3 pounds, 14 ounces she was about six weeks premature. I needed to be there and it was killing me I wasn't. Each pay period I sent money home to help pay the bills and to bank for the fall but it wasn't the same. So Monday morning I let my manager know I needed to go. I was shocked to hear from them they thought my leaving was a mistake and I was likely burning bridges- but I didn't care. Family had to come first.

Car packed, I headed home. Did it negatively impact the project? In the big picture, not really. By the way, this thought that the business has to come over family is prevalent in many parts of the business world. Brace yourself.

Lesson: The likelihood is good you will work for many companies throughout your career and you'll be forced here or there to leave a company to act in your family's best interest. The Sun will rise tomorrow and if you're a good engineer you'll find work again easily. So don't sweat it. Always put your family first.

The Chocolate Santa Clause

Noted American author Samuel Clemens, better known by his pen name Mark Train, once said "Truth is stranger than fiction, but it is because fiction is obliged to stick to possibilities; truth isn't." Likewise, as you grow up you're going to hear a news commentator or friend say about a story, "You just can't make this stuff up." What they are referring to is the ironic fact that some things are so unbelievable they have to be true. And from an alternative-reality perspective, they can make perfect sense- *weird stuff happens.*

In my final semester at Norfolk State University one of my classes was Statistics II. The second in the calculus-based series, its professor was a diminutive, very professional-looking gentleman in his sixties. Google searches and more digging than I care to admit haven't yielded his name but I will say he was one of the smartest and funniest instructors there. He was popular among faculty throughout the university, was always connected into upcoming cultural and social events, and happily encouraged student participation from the perspective it would help us grow socially and intellectually. Hearing in his voice and seeing in his eyes his recommendations came from-the-heart, I couldn't help but like the guy.

This professor's sense of humor showed itself in interesting ways. He could tell when our eyes were beginning to glaze over as we discussed nonparametric statistics, a.k.a. rebels without a distribution, and adeptly challenged us with problems to which we could relate. Knowing we were mostly single people in our early twenties, he regularly started a problem with, "Let's say you and your friends are going out to the club to dance. X percent of the beautiful ladies there would like to meet a gentleman with light-colored eyes, Y percent prefer a great smile, now let's determine the likelihood..." We'd laugh, he'd laugh, and instantly we were reengaged. Many of his backgrounds for puzzles demonstrated real world application. However, when it came to the math of it all, he was dead dog serious.

He also liked to say, "I consider myself a Chocolate Santa Claus. If I can see your thinking is on the right path I may give you the benefit of the doubt. But don't come up to me after a test to tell me I made a mistake grading your paper as I will find those points someplace else." We had great respect for that outlook as it offered the thought there is some balance in life; even in mathematics everything wasn't black or white. That having been written, Statistics II was no joke- it took the algebra and calculus we'd learned to this point, built upon it, and then applied it to real world problems. If there was a mathematics equivalent to the lab courses students took in physics and chemistry this was it. And it was great fun.

Now back to our friend Mark Twain and how the unlikely made perfect sense. Earlier in this book you learned Navy guys traditionally like to mess with each other; because they're friends. In a deliciously-evil and funny way our professor turned the tables on us and it was indeed stranger than fiction.

On my last academic day at Norfolk State I had the pleasure of enduring a two hour, fifty-question, show-your-work, Statics II final exam. I arrived with three, expertly-sharpened number two pencils ready to do battle. Our professor was wearing one of his best three piece suits and carrying the more than one hundred page, Sunday edition of the Washington Post newspaper. He was ready too.

It was yet another hot, ninety-degree day in Norfolk, Virginia and our classroom had no air conditioning. The windows were slightly cracked-open, upwardly, in old-school fashion but this provided little relief. As the professor passed out the exams he had an odd smile on his face but we chocked it up to it being our last day. And I had studied hard, very hard in fact, and was ready for anything.

The questions were multiple choice but we had to show your work. Question 1, almost a gimmie, the answer was "A"; work shown. Question 2, a bit of a teaser but if one studied he got it and also "A"; work shown. Question 3 the same "A" and on it went till question 8, also "A." It was at this point I gazed down at my answer sheet and started getting a little nervous. Questions 9, 10, and 11 also all "A." Okay, enough! I looked up at him and half held up my hand. As one of his better students he knew what I was going to ask, tilted his head, and slightly waved his index finger like a small-car windshield wiper as if to say, "I know your suspicious but don't even ask that question." His authoritative expression slowly turned to a grin and he lifted the Entertainment section of the paper up so I couldn't see is face. There was no way in heck, statistically, these answers should all have been "A." However I had studied, knew these answers were right, and also felt if he were crafty enough to do this he was also crafty enough to not go the full fifty questions with it.

This professor's gremlin-like machination had sent a full shockwave of fear through most of the future engineers and computer scientists taking the exam. Deep breaths and sighs could be heard here and there among my classmates. I felt it in the room as surely as I feel the hair on my arm stand on end whenever a thunderstorm creeps in. Head down, I kept going. Sure enough, at question 40 the answer was "B." Cute. At this point I figured all bets were off and it would turn into a normal test. Nope.

Questions 40 through 50 all had the answer "B." Of course we still had to show our work but his test was still as devious as devious could be- giving an advanced statistics final exam of 50 questions where 40 were "A" and 10 "B." The likelihood of that is, well, just as likely as any other distribution until humans get involved. However, in the real world test makers have the tendency to choose options that include all of the multiple choice answers in a more random sequence.

A few days later I went to visit him and to get my grade. It was a 98. I had goofed up a couple points around notation that took me out into the weeds. When I asked him about the test he said, "I knew you figured something fishy was up but I couldn't have you make this surprise known. Do you know some folks actually gambled all 50 answers were "A"? And they went to great lengths to prove in their last 10 answers that "A" was correct." We both shared a good laugh and deep down I breathed a sigh of relief. In that moment he too had become a favorite uncle. We had connected on an academic and intellectual level; something rare yet special. This professor was smart, great at keeping us engaged, and really enjoyed his profession. In your calling, whatever it may become, this is the kind of Zen worthy of seeking; a personal expression of insight in your daily life especially for the benefit of others.

Lesson: We can study facts, figures, and equations till the sun goes down. At the end of the day we cannot deny the penchant for someone to stay true to his nature. If he is usually a serious person, the likelihood is high he'll be that way in the future. If he is playful or unconventional, that too is something you'll likely see again. This inability of most humans to adapt or change their ways from serious to playful or the other way around becomes more pronounced as we get older. Every once in a while you'll encounter someone who has mastered the ability to be both at the same time. Learn as much as you can from him for he is usually the most happy of people and has the most worthy lessons to teach; educationally and socially.

Let It Rain Pennies From Heaven

In the spring and fall of each year, across America, universities host career fairs or expos. Both private sector companies and public, government agencies attend to give future graduates an opportunity to learn more about them. They are always interested in meeting engineers but their interests in students of other majors vary with the state of the market and the organization's needs. Remember when I mentioned employers love "curve breakers"? At the Norfolk State career fair, this is where that was proven true.

Each company table I visited had nice brochures, smiling representatives, and a paper listing requirements of the candidates they sought. For example, computer science, computer engineering, or electrical engineering majors with a GPA of 3.0 or better were in very high demand. Three companies covering the engineering spectrum are worthy of mention because they were easy to compare and contrast.

The first was the United States government's Bureau of Weights and Measures. Their representatives were professional in demeanor, provided nice brochures, but for the life of me I couldn't feel inspired by their mission of promoting equity in all commercial transactions based on weight or measure. It seemed to be to science what ensuring all printed materials using a color called "brown" precisely matched the RGB value of (165, 42, 0) ..was to science. Okay, we've locked in that concept. Now what?

At the time, they were seeking engineers or information systems graduates with a GPA of 2.0 or better. As you navigate through high school and especially college you'll come to do some group projects and you won't always get to choose your team members. Some on your team will be curve breakers; ones who look at an assignment like it's a present on Christmas morning and just can't wait to have at it. Some others will do a decent "B" level job. Then they'll be those bringing up the rear and just going through the motions. This latter bunch are the ones you'll have to keep asking, "Did you get your part done? When can we expect to see the initial draft?" They are the ones for whom you'll end up covering and the ones who, in the end, will cause your team grade to fall from an "A" to a "B" because of their "C-" level effort. This is the 2.0 crowd. I definitely consider myself an "effort snob." And to me, grades are a documentation of the effectiveness of one's effort. So, at the end of the day you have to ask yourself whether or not you want to work for an organization hiring and likely managed by 2.0 GPA people. The Bureau of Weights and Measures mission has value in the commercial world, however, it's one of making sure things run correctly. Being a person of incessant curiosity and high energy, I wanted to be out on the edge- where new things are created. So, respectfully, I passed them by.

AT&T was another company. They had cultivated contacts with our faculty and already knew the best students; those with a GPA of 3.5 or better. A few of us had been chatted up about how it was an engineer's dream to work with AT&T, that we should check them out, and we were personally invited to two events. The first was a formal dinner at a very nice restaurant. The second, an informal pizza party.

At the dinner event I was almost giddy with excitement. We all wore suits and sat tall in our chairs. There was candlelight, fancy white dinner napkins, light music in the background; a dreamlike and surreal environment to someone who six hours before had happily eaten a discounted 7-11 spicy bean burrito. I was careful to use the salad fork with the salad, kept track of which was my water glass, didn't talk with food in my mouth- you know, the basics. I was on the verge of realizing something big and deep down, I was a nervous wreck.

The AT&T team was great at keeping the conversation light and friendly- talking about the company, the way they were a nice family, and the many paths the career of an engineer could take. It sounded almost magical. The evening went off smoothly and towards the end they mentioned they were going to host an informal pizza party the next night to which we were all invited. This next event was an effort to show they weren't always wearing suits and knew how to laugh and enjoy more casual time as well.

Overall the AT&T approach to meeting prospective team members was flawless and I'm sure I would have enjoyed an amazing career with this top-shelf company. However the wonderful thing I discovered, and you will too should you choose to become an engineer, is there is an almost unlimited number of companies and career paths one could take. The third company with whom I met is generally secretive despite having been in the news recently- the National Security Agency or NSA.

Having a U. S. Navy crypto background makes one a really smart match for the NSA. Located at Ft. Meade, Maryland, their headquarters is midway between the exciting cultural and historical things to do in Washington, D.C. and the beautiful Maryland beaches. Naturally, I found myself drawn to them.

Their representatives wore nice suits and not the stereotypical London Fog trench coat one might expect when meeting members of the world's preeminent spy agency. They smiled, were personable, and looked almost as if they were expecting me when I said hello. I handed them my resume and they smiled even more. Then, grinning, I asked them to tell me what the NSA did. They stated, "The organization's core missions are to protect U.S. national security systems and to produce foreign signals intelligence information." "Yes," I said, "but how do you do it?" An even larger smile came across their faces and then they gave me the tilted head look as if to say, "You're really going to ask us that question?"

Quickly the conversation shifted to the opportunity to work with the latest technologies, their encouragement of employees to advance their education at the graduate level, and the idea the NSA was a fun place to work. After my filling out an application and their requesting my transcripts, I was invited to visit Ft. Meade that weekend and interview. I couldn't resist.

Of course, running up to Ft. Meade, Maryland the next day did cost me the AT&T pizza party but to me this was a much bigger deal if you know what I mean. They brought me up and paid for the hotel. I shared a room with an Army guy also interviewing or he could have been a plant to see how chatty I'd be about my United States Navy exploits; I have no idea. Now I'm not a conspiracy theory guy but as a math minor I appreciate the statistical likelihoods of certain things being true. If I were them I'd surely want to collect all the information I could when deciding whether or not to entrust someone with the nation's most important secrets. Again, I have no *proof* that was the case here.

The interview process with the NSA was a full day event. We interviewed with people, received a tour, took several academic tests, and even enjoyed one-on-one sessions with a psychiatrist. Some of the tests were general logic and some specifically about my computer science major. However the most interesting question of the entire day came from the psychiatrist. He asked, "Do you think the ends justify the means?"

Now there's a philosophical question for the ages- something we could talk about for hours. What I do appreciate is the reason for asking the question. NSA employees can have access to very sensitive, compartmentalized information that if divulged could put those working for or with the United States in grave danger and even harm the country itself. So when hiring, it's important to try to understand what's going on inside an applicant's mind.

The interview went well and they generally offered someone at my level $32,500 to start. In 2017 dollars it's roughly $71,142. Not bad for someone with a simple bachelor's of science degree.

The next step was for them to analyze my test results and let me know. Leaving, I felt a very positive vibe almost as if I'd found my home. For the next couple of days I was looking at the real estate section of the Ft. Meade area newspapers for places to live and trying to learn about the different communities. Being towards the end of my second senior year semester, I still visited my department to say hello and had an odd feeling. It was a feeling of impending loss as I knew the remaining time with my now beloved Norfolk State family was growing small.

Walking to attend our last semester meeting of the Norfolk State Association For Computing Machinery, I happened to notice one more full page note on the department bulletin board. A company called E-Systems was interviewing for computer science positions in Northern Virginia. E-Systems?! I'd seen the name before but where? And then it came to me. E-Systems had manufactured some of the specialized gear we'd used in the Navy. Excitedly, I scribbled down the information and stuffed it into my worn-out wrangler jeans pocket.

As soon as I got home I picked up the phone. My heart raced at the prospect of supporting my brothers and sisters still in the service at a much higher level as I dialed the number. I mentioned my name, where I saw their note, and that I was interested. They said they were going to be in Virginia Beach next week, provided all the information I needed to bring, and scheduled my interview.

Arriving in my one and only suit, buffed yet completely worn black dress shoes, and in big need of a haircut I held my head high and did my best. They were a team of three; one senior developer and two managers. The questions started slowly and then the pace picked up. Tell us the languages you've learned, which classes you liked best, the difference between object code and binary, the value of separating interface and database code, why compiled code runs faster than scripts, the challenges you noticed in building voice recognition software in your senior project. I felt like a young Mr. Spock being pinged one question after the next at the Vulcan Academy Of Science on finals day. Again though, my U.S. Navy training experience helped me maintain my composure and I was able to nail every technical and organizational question they threw my way. I had nothing to lose- and everything to gain. Inside I was almost laughing in thinking, "That's all you've got?"

Towards the end of the interview we came to the money part of the discussion. Being a commercial company they had some flexibility on how they packaged compensation; as compared to some government organizations with stricter pay scales. They asked with whom I had interviewed. Being in full bluff mode, I told them General Electric, AT&T, and the NSA. Skipping the first two, they immediately asked, "So what did the NSA offer you?"

There was no way not to smile at that question. How did they know the NSA would be my first choice? I imagine it was because of my positive feelings towards my U. S. Navy experience and that type of work. Without hesitation I tossed out, "$32,500" even though the NSA had made no offer yet. Negotiating for salary is an art and a game much like poker. They don't know what offers you have and you don't know how big a compensation package they'll offer. So I was bluffing big time.

Their response, "Give us a second." They conferred privately for a minute and then sat back down. "How would you like to work with us and start at $36,500?" I stood up, extended my hand, and with a big smile said, "I'd be honored to be a part of your team." Done deal.

Suddenly I'd gone from scraping by below poverty at $9,500 per year to nearly four times that amount. You'll hear from time to time of people becoming an overnight success. In this case it took me one failed year of college, four years of U.S. Navy experience plus four years of solid college effort to become an overnight success. Although you don't need the service experience I think it really helps. It demonstrates your ability to function within an organization, to be disciplined in your actions, and it teaches you to both follow and lead.

Lesson: Good grades open doors to opportunities beyond your wildest belief. Engineers, especially software engineers, are needed in every walk of life. You could support a non-profit organization, a commercial one, or one of the many governmental departments. Focus on your grades and you'll be in the driver's seat come graduation to choose what you like.

Survival Style Points

Some people are fortunate to have plenty of money for food, clothing, rent, tuition, and more. And some aren't. If you have limited means you may need to be creative in making it through. Please don't let pride or what anyone else thinks stand between you and your objective. What others think in the more challenging times of your life pales in comparison to value of the self-confidence you'll gain by pushing forward. So just hold your head high and go for it.

While attending college in the daytime, I worked at 7-11 nights. One store was very close to Old Dominion University where some of the more arrogant, rich students would come to buy cheap beer, wine, and gigunda-sized bags of Doritos. The other store in which I worked was in a very rough, poor neighborhood where we were robbed repeatedly- me, personally, three times. Company policy was to let them take what they wanted and not resist. So we did, hoping they'd focus on what they were taking and not kill us where we stood. Night after night I'd make coffee, Slurpees, Big Bite hot dogs, clean the cheese and chili dispensers, lug in seventy pound soda syrup cylinders, restock the cooler, count money, restock the shelves, and more. And we did it all with a smile. Sometimes I'd even bring books in for study as between 2 AM and 4 AM the only customers were regular truck drivers getting coffee. It was not uncommon for me to be in a but-for-me empty store at 3:15 AM with candy bars to my left, gooey cheese dispenser to my right, and the Calculus III book opened up right in the middle. *That's commitment.*

Our budget for food was limited; usually $35 for two people for an entire week. We bought chicken thighs- the cheapest cut available, vegetables, one dozen eggs, Kool-Aid, tea bags, and sugar; which we used in half amounts the Kool-Aid package suggested. Down the street was the bakery thrift store we visited, the place they would bring discounted bread products close to their expiration dates. Over time, we found some awesome tricks- things people these days might call a poor-person's life hacks.

Our 7-11 store had an enclosed display case full of fancy pastries, muffins, and doughnuts- items way outside our budget. Each morning at 4 AM the Dunkin Doughnuts delivery man would come by, take out his clipboard, write off the day old items, and toss them into the trash. Then he'd refill the case. And one night, as I watched those expensive goodies tumble into the trashcan, it dawned on me. I snagged a brand new plastic trash bag, held it out and said, "Let me help you with that." He knew I was working my way through school, tilted his head, smiled, and was happy to oblige. Soon our fridge and freezer were well stocked with day-old, tasty breakfast treats.

The same was true with those half-pound 7-11 burritos. Okay, stop laughing. Yes you. *Zip it.* It's true, absent scanning the back of a burrito package with a universal chemical translator no one really knows what's inside those things. Still they provided sustenance. The business process was simple. I'd take the burritos out of the freezer, set the print date five days forward, place stickers on the burritos, and put them into the case. When a burrito in the case was at the date on the package, it could no longer be sold to the public. I was very careful to follow the store rules about proper inventory, but past the expiration date they went into a plastic trash bag and straight to my home.

Over time one does learn to assimilate microwaveable burritos, however, I must confess there were moments it felt it was a race between the burrito's fervent desire to decompose and my body's need to extract nutrients. Let me give a shout out right now to the makers of Sodium Diacetate for its awesome flavoring and antimicrobial properties. *I haven't twitched in years.*

If you are fortunate enough to live within walking distance of your college or have access to affordable public transportation, congratulations! If not, you may need to get creative in this area too. While in the Navy we were lucky enough to find a little old lady wanting to junk a car for $1. It was a forest green, 1967 Plymouth Valiant. New tires were $40 each. The engine was the very easy to maintain Slant-6. I could change the oil, air filter, and spark plugs myself. And we carried spare parts from the junk yard in the trunk just in case. This $1 model though had some issues.

None of the door locks worked and two of the windows would not roll down. The driver's seat had springs popping up through it and an inverted coat hanger served as the radio antenna. The driver's side back door was smashed closed due to an impact. And the hub caps were removed because they would cut the valve stems, where the air goes in, causing the tires to go flat. So how does one survive the abject humiliation of being seen in such a vehicle? You focus on your greater purpose- the reason for being there. *Nothing covers a poor person's cloak of humiliation better than earning outstanding grades in school. The classroom is the great equalizer.* Just hold your head high and keep moving forward. Trust me in this. Please trust me.

This little car served me well for four full years and my most favorite moment in it came on a very warm day in the first week of May, 1990. It was my last day of final exams in my final semester. I put my car on a grassy knoll that served as overflow parking and headed in for the first test. Having studied hard, I wasn't concerned. Ninety minutes later I emerged, exhilarated, with only one test remaining and an hour to kill. The outdoor thermometer was pegging ninety degrees and I was hot, thirsty, and broke. Walking up to my pitted with rust, green Valiant I noticed something odd. There were shiny, black BMW's parked on each side of it and someone had placed a crisp, new $1 bill under my windshield- a pity offering from the rich kids- and a very good joke.

Taking the $1 I zipped over to 7-11, purchased a frosty-cold cherry Slurpee, and parked back in my spot. After ten minutes my upper-crust, Guess-jean-wearing benefactors arrived, pointing and giggling as I proudly sat atop the hood of old faithful; Slurpee-holding arm raised in a toast to them. As they drove off I too had to laugh. One hundred five minutes later I had crushed the last final- advanced calculus-based statistics. And that was one tasty Slurpee.

Lesson: Be strong, fearless, creative, persistent, polite, and oblivious to what others think of you when pursuing your dream. In time you will succeed.

We Said Hello Goodbye

Graduation day at Norfolk State University was the culmination of a lot of hard work. One thousand four hundred sixty one days had passed since I took the leap of faith to leverage U.S. Navy experience in the classroom. There had been thousands of hours of study, lots of fretting over upcoming tests, and big smiles from our now favorite aunts and uncles when we demonstrated knowledge. Over nine hundred of us marched that day, dressed nicely, in front of family and friends. For each of us though, life was about to change. When you are a senior in college, especially in your last semester, you walk the campus head held high almost like you own the place. You've mastered your major and it feels like you know everything and virtually everyone. This level of Zen frees you to notice things you hadn't in your first few years- the morning sun painting the bricks of your favorite buildings, the dew on the grass, the freshness of the air; everything. Although graduation day is an amazing thing, it's also a discrete event, a moment in time that comes and goes. And beyond it is the next great unknown.

After achieving an important goal it's natural to experience a letdown, and moving forward almost a feeling of loss. That's how it felt for me on graduation day. It dawned on me I wasn't coming back the next week, I wasn't going to lug books and my mushed-up peanut butter and jelly sandwich across campus, and I wouldn't again enjoy the mentoring of my favorite professors- ever.

So for me graduation was a weird combination of satisfaction and somberness. Wearing the cap and gown felt nice and one by one I began to see all my favorite professors up on stage. Each had mentored me in different areas; science, career paths, politics, and human nature. And as my turn came to walk on stage to accept my diploma they were all smiling. To the side, one gentleman caught my eye. It was my football coach, Mr. Tom Morris. He didn't say a word but gave a simple nod of the head and a smile. That single gesture spoke volumes and reaffirmed all the real, useful, life advice he had offered over the years. Sometimes the most basic friendships are truly endearing and his was one of those.

After the graduation ceremony we were all invited back to the Math & Computer Science Department office for a little party of cake and champagne. What? Liquor on campus.. in the Dean's office? Okay. It was a chance to celebrate and say our goodbyes. Everyone was fidgeting with excitement, talking about where they were going next, and our professors were encouraging us to call by them by their first names. But I just couldn't do it. Some professors earn a deep respect and reverence that remains forever. For Dr. DeLoatch and Dr. Harrison it was just that way. They would always be *Doctor* and just speaking their title made me feel good. With cake and champagne in hand then, and I say virtually now, "Thank you Doctors. Your generously given gifts of wisdom, encouragement, and professional example prepared me for the great adventure that was to follow. "

Lesson: When you realize a big goal such as graduating from college do enjoy the moment for it may never come again. The trick to happiness is what you do next. Keep coming up with interesting, challenging, and fun things you want to do. Create a new set of personal and professional goals. Then make your plans to realize those. And just go for it. In life, this can keep you feeling young.

By Tom Nicholas

PART V: MY SURVEY OF TODAY'S LANDSCAPE

Will Your Choice Of School Matter?

Prior to the year 2000, a notion that high-quality engineering education was a scarce resource had been perpetuated by a handful of universities. They were and are *businesses* and the limited ability of humans to share knowledge in real time contributed to the fact there were a relatively small number of places with limited amounts of student space. Advance to the year 2014 and we saw, referencing the *Straighterline.com Brief History Of Online Learning* article, over 98% of colleges offer online courses. This amazing reality means anyone, anywhere with an internet connection can obtain a great education. Do you live in Peoria, Illinois and want to earn a degree in information technology from the University Of Massachusetts Lowell? Perhaps you live in Karapur, India and want to earn a degree in computer science from the University Of Florida? Or maybe, you live in Rocky Mount, North Carolina and would like to earn your bachelor's degree in software engineering from Arizona State University? No problem- just open your web browser, navigate to their respective website, and get started.

Another good byproduct of this disruption to post-secondary education is competition. Now that so many college and university degree programs are available online, prices are becoming much more affordable. Scarcity as it relates to access has virtually become a thing of the past. And now it will, as it should, come down to the knowledge of the candidate himself when it comes to hiring.

So does the choice of the school matter? Let me tell you, having filled the role of technical lead and engineering manager I've hired many, many developers. *Neither I nor the other professionals with whom I've worked put a lot of stock in the name of the school listed on a person's resume. What matters most is whether or not the person has a solid skill set and possesses positive, team-oriented energy ready to be applied.*

It's at this point we need to talk a little about Nano degrees and non-college-degree technical training.

Nano-degrees and other less well-rounded technical training *alone* can get a person into an entry-level programmer position but this minimalist education could leave him at eventual employment risk due to competition.

Let's say a United States-based Nano degree holder is hired and is being paid at $80,000. With vacation time, medical, and other benefits let's push that total value to $100,000. One of the many truths in this world is that public companies exist to make a profit for their shareholders- they aren't community charity organizations. They want high-quality work at the lowest cost possible. On the surface it might appear the Nano degree holder could be a perfect fit for this. However, let me tell you what I'm seeing in the field today.

From a financial perspective, we work with three types of engineers:

- First, our own, American citizen employee engineers. We always look to hire people with four-year degrees because, although not plentiful, they are available. We've never reached the point where we chose to hire someone who didn't have a full degree and that thinking is because we like cultivating our engineers into future company leaders. Of course, some American companies surely hire Nano-degree folks; we just haven't yet.

- Next, we've established relationships with Asian consulting companies- some in India and some in China. These engineers are capable of solid work provided they are given very high-quality requirements and there is good feedback and guidance throughout the project. In our experience, working with Asian consulting companies is the most cost-effective, most profitable option, and we have been moving to them more and more. We generally have no idea whether or not their employees have full degrees or Nano-degrees. We just know they work cheaply and do a good job.

- Lastly, when we have no other choice, we'll hire United States-based, local consultants. We put out bids for work to consulting companies with which we have relationships, agree to short term contracts, provide specifications, and drive the software development lifecycle with them. American-based consultants are the highest-educated, most expensive, least profitable path for us so we try to avoid using them.

Therefore, an American Nano degree employee is less qualified than someone with a four-year engineering degree and more expensive than our Asian consultants. So people in this category can find themselves in a tough spot unless they work hard to build up their people skills and establish good business relationships within their company. In my opinion, the best thing a Nano degree person can do is to take the money he is making and immediately use it to complete his formal college degree in his off hours. *In determining which technical person to promote to the next level within an organization, having a four-year engineering degree is oftentimes a determining factor.*

If you noticed above, I hinted that a Nano degree *alone* isn't enough. However, a Nano degree can help an employee who already has a non-technical degree completely reinvent himself. If a person found himself in a department where people having his specialty were in over-abundance, he could complete a Nano degree program and serve in a technical capacity going forward or just for some time. He could then leverage that experience to transition to new work in his company. For example, let's say a person with a degree in accounting or finance knew his company was going to shift to a new software package and that would eventually trigger department reorganization. It could then be in his interest to acquire a Nano degree or training that would teach him how to configure or customize that new system. And then when the company made the shift to it, he'd be in a sweet spot for a position with enhanced responsibilities.

Meet The Players

When you take a deeper look into virtually every profession, you'll learn they are organized into levels of experience and specializations. This is very much true in the world of software development. And you're going to work with non-technical people who will have no clue of these differentiations within the world of software. Part of your ongoing mission will be to create elegant technical solutions. The other part will be to diplomatically mentor and interact with your uninitiated coworkers.

It's completely normal as part of the adventure for an engineer to transition from programmer/coder to any and all of the positions I'm about to describe. In the following sections I list common titles, discuss the role of the person within the organization, the people with whom he interacts, and sometimes hint at whether or not he works in his own office. Why would having an office matter?

Nearly every engineer I've met needs a quiet environment to do his best work. Some of the time having one's own office isn't logistically possible due to lack of space. Other times old-time thinking managers see an office as a prize awarded to people who have been with the organization a long time and have earned the privilege. However, whether or not an engineer is in his own office it's clear a quiet environment helps.

Additionally, in parts of this book I interchangeably use the titles "software developer," "developer," "software engineer," and "engineer." The differentiation is esoteric and I mostly interchange them as a preference over using "developer" four times in three consecutive sentences. Without further ado, here are some personal observations based on real world experiences!

The Programmer/Coder

"Programmer" or the less professional "coder" is oftentimes the first position into which a new person with a computer science or information systems degree will be hired. Usually having less than two years' experience and as the junior member of the team, the programmer is mentored or guided by developers and software engineers on the team, his manager, project managers, and virtually everyone else in the organization. Although he may have decent development skills, there is so much more which he must learn to rise within the organization. These items include, but are not limited to: business etiquette, effective communication, dressing for success, the value of hard work, applied computer science theory, coding conventions employed by the organization, source code backup and storage procedures, protocols for unit and integration testing, formal QA, moving applications and databases into production environments, and much more. Some of these aspects are taught in college. However, most people acquire them over time in the real business world.

Most of the time a programmer reviews specifications documents *after* they have been created by more experienced team members such as architects, software engineers, or business analysts / technical project managers. In larger projects he is assigned to build smaller components such as individual web pages, class methods, or database stored procedures. In smaller projects or within smaller companies he may have the opportunity to collect the requirements, write the specifications, and build the entire thing; end to end.

Many companies seat their programmers in cubicle areas where they can support each other. In some cases they do get their own offices, however, in my experience this is very rare. A challenge you are going to face is that cubicle areas are not known for being quiet and the noise can be a distraction you'll need to endure and overcome.

The Software Developer

The software developer is the next senior position after programmer and in my opinion there are two types; the good ones who aspire to become software engineers and those who have reached their career peak and have become "slackers." The good ones have a few years' experience and have completed several if not dozens of successful projects or invested significant time maintaining existing systems. They suggest process improvement ideas and build solid, reusable class code. Company management, project managers, and other software developers trust them and come to them as resources to answer status and "what if" type questions related to the business or organization's activities. This is especially true in smaller companies where software developers have the opportunity to play many roles; oftentimes in parallel.

Good software developers mentor programmers too; teaching them departmental-level things they need to know to be effective members of the team. It's also at this level where the developer begins to have his eyes opened to how the organization really functions, beyond the company's glossy brochures and published organizational charts, and he begins to consider whether he wishes to pursue a purely technical career path or move into management.

In smaller organizations software developers participate in conference calls with clients, partner companies, and vendors as well. Over time they sync up with managers and more senior members on such calls- and this is where great team chemistry is built. It is a lot like high school sports or even band- you begin to play with a team and realize together you can do some great things. As time goes by, you want to work with them and want them on your team. It's also where the good software developer begins to realize which team members need more support and he willingly lends a hand to help them become better.

The second class of software developer is the "slacker." *And he is the most dangerous person in the organization.* His lack of attention to detail and minimal effort can cause stress, organizational chaos, and damage that ripples through the company lowering morale and risking the entire business. Let's consider a hypothetical slacker and his attributes.

Say we have a slacker team member, call him Jake. Jake shows up to work ten or twenty minutes late every day. Half the time he's messing with his fantasy football selections, day trading stocks, checking out the office hotties, or wasting time on Facebook. Jake knows which departments put out free doughnuts on certain days, he is always the first person in line at the company ice cream social, and at the holiday party he swoops in on the bacon-wrapped scallops like an aggressive, half-starved seagull. Jake drinks a little too much, talks about how "The Man is keeping him down," and makes cringe-worthy inappropriate comments about his coworkers because he's just *keepin-it-real.*

He shows up late to team and project meetings, never brings a notepad and pen, and half pays attention. Whenever Jake is asked a question he deflects it; giving an answer with so many caveats it's worthless. Jake doesn't volunteer new ideas but he shoots down every idea given by others. Jake's code sucks- he doesn't create technical process flow diagrams, doesn't schema out his database first, doesn't wrap his stored procedures in transactions, doesn't add useful code comments, celebrates unmaintainable obfuscation in his methods thinking it provides job security, and thinks inheritance is something his parents are going to give him when they die.

Jake likes to work off the grid- preferring to use his own tools and own laptop when he can get away with it. He has to be reminded to check in his code and there is some of it he can't even find. Jake's deliverables, the parts of a project for which he is responsible, are never on time. And when they are delivered they are of poor quality.

Jake doesn't do unit testing and you only learn this when you are trying to integration test with him. So you have to help him unit test and find and fix his bugs- the things he calls "undocumented features." This in turn makes the project late; torqueing off the project manager, senior management, and the client. And when questioned about it, Jake will inevitably find a way to throw you under the bus to take some of the blame.

Jake is the most disliked, obtuse piece of flotsam you will ever encounter and if Human Resources could find a way to get rid of him they would in a heartbeat. ***Don't be Jake.***

The Software Consultant

The software consultant is an interesting position to say the least. These are often more senior people, experts if you will, in specific areas brought in when companies either don't have that expertise or are overwhelmed with work and are having a tough time keeping up.

There are two types of consultants: ones who are employed by a consulting company and ones who have their own, usually small company. Consultant's roles are defined by a document the hiring company, perhaps your company, writes called a Statement Of Work or S.O.W. The S.O.W. defines the particular project or projects on which the consultant will work, deliverables, timelines, types of tools and expertise to be used, pricing, and standard regulatory and governing terms.

Good consultants are great at their craft and also excellent diplomats. They recognize, for example, when competing opinions exist within their client company and step back for things to get sorted out before proceeding. In a perfect world, companies using consultants have their project plan and requirements completed before the consultant arrives. And the consultant comes in like a surgeon, performs his specific tasks, and then leaves. *In my twenty-plus years I've never seen it go that way; usually because companies choose not to invest the time to get that organized before bringing the consultant aboard.*

As a consultant, you want to fit into the culture of the hiring company. You aren't an employee but you are an important member of the team. Successful consultants show deference and kindness to everyone in their client companies not only because politeness is good but because client personnel can be your best friend or they could work to end your contract should they feel mistreated. As the consultant adds value to the project he begins to make friends and they begin to treat him as part of the team- inviting him to lunch, happy hours, and other kinds of things. Sometimes S.O.W.s also specify, contractually, a way for the consultant to become an employee of the hiring company after some probationary time.

The consultant is definitely a *techno-diplomat* and can have a fun time in this position. He keeps his head on a swivel politically; keeping track of how the organization operates and who within it influences its direction. He gets paid whether the hiring company utilizes his great suggestions or not, whether they profit in the long term or not. However, consulting gigs don't last as long as full time positions. Having been a consultant and having owned two of my own companies for over eight years, I've worked dozens of contracts. Some of these lasted for just a month or two and some for more than a year. It can be exciting and rewarding, however, one never really knows when a contract will end so banking money during each contract is important.

The Systems Analyst And Business Analyst

Systems analysts are oftentimes referred to as efficiency experts. They look at how things are currently being done, come up with alternatives, and present them to management for consideration. If management approves them, the systems analyst could be assigned to lead implementation of those ideas. The systems analyst experience-wise is somewhere between a software developer and an architect. Depending upon the organization, he may exclusively support his internal team or he may be loaned out to other departments to bridge the technical skills gap between that department and his. These analysts also investigate and explore how new technologies or partner-company systems could integrate with your systems and they prepare reports with recommendations.

Business analysts participate in meetings to help map high-level business needs to technical ones either within or across systems. By that I mean they take non-technical requests from business people and translate them into technical requirements documents which include *use cases* and *process flows* describing user types, the order in which things need to happen, and systems involved. Being an analyst can be an exciting position if you enjoy working with people and helping to solve puzzles.

The Software Engineer

The next level in experience and ability after software developer is the software engineer. Those at this level have participated in what is known as the full SDLC; software development life cycle. SDLC events include requirements analysis, web site or application design, development of front end interfaces (screens) as well as middle ware (classes) and databases, the backing up of code, unit testing, integration testing, support of or participation in the quality assurance (QA) process, deployment to production environments, ongoing operations support, creation of training materials, and training of the user community. The likelihood is high the software engineer has done all of these things in his career. He keeps up with advances in technology, trends, and knows his organization's needs well.

Software engineers often mentor other developers as well as junior project managers and they regularly consult with senior project managers (PMs) and participate in technical feasibility discussions with senior management in providing them information critical to their decision making.

As you would guess, these kinds of activities require great diplomacy skills. Good software engineers are free of technology bias in that they keep an open mind when presenting options. They are aware virtually every technical challenge has more than one possible solution and they are adept at presenting the pros and cons of each. In the organization they are oftentimes referred to as the company expert or guru as it relates to particular applications or technologies. Really good software engineers don't let this go to their heads. Instead they present a modest and respectful profile; making them even more liked within their company. With these added responsibilities and abilities, it is common for software engineers to have their own office. It doesn't always happen but it is quite common.

The Architect

Architects are designers of more complex, frequently multi-platform, applications and databases. They are usually employed by large organizations and consulting companies and less so by small to mid-sized ones. In a Star Wars terms, they are more like Yoda and less like Luke.

In larger organizations architects are very senior people loaned out to different departments for their expertise. Most of the time, they work in their own office. In mid-sized to smaller organizations senior software engineers often do this same kind of design work as well as development.

Architects regularly participate in meetings with senior management on longer term strategic technology initiatives. And they often conduct independent research and present their findings to their organization. So obviously, skills in diplomacy and public speaking are important for architects too.

The Solution Architect

Of all the positions available to senior engineers, the solution architect is probably my favorite and the one I consider the most valuable to a company. Helping the organization realize its goal of making efficient use of resources is where the solution architect can really shine. In our line of work the terms "upstream" and "downstream" come into play quite a bit. Upstream is as close to the customer or user as possible and downstream means further and further away from where data originates. Silly logic, junk data, and other yucky things drain more money, cause more engineering pain, and represent more risk to the company the further downstream they exist so solution architects create inter-system process flows that try to prevent this. In addition to his engineering skills, the solution architect must know his company's capabilities and systems inside out and backwards. He must have a deep understanding of the internal processes for running the business as well as the human and software interfaces in communicating with clients, partners, and customers.

The job of the solution architect is to work with sales people, clients, and partners in capturing correct, feasible, necessary, unambiguous, testable, complete, and traceable business requirements. This also means his job is to help thwart every ill-conceived, uninformed, wish-list notion that violates the tenants of "good requirements."

You may be able to tell I've got a little pent up energy on this particular topic. It comes from years of working with sales people who have had the collective attention span of a family of underfed New York City tree squirrels. Now they aren't all like this, however, many are. During requirements conversations, this particular species of sales person tends to filibuster or go on without letting you ask questions and drops in incoherent phrases like, "They're going to move the thing to the place and yada-yada-yada, stuff happens and everybody's happy. Right-right-right. Let's move on."

Soft skills required to effectively support the underfed New York City tree squirrel are rarely built into the genetic code of the common engineer because these aren't binary attributes. They're more like artificial intelligence (AI) algorithms; developed over time with project experience. When dealing with clients, sales people must be flexible because client needs are determined through flowing conversations. *This means they often convince clients to buy things they never knew they always wanted.* Marinate on that for a second.

The sales person's world itself isn't a finite set of one and zero, options but rather a stream of "what if" and "how about" conversations which are strung together to form "I'll agree to that" statements of work.

The solution architect engages diplomatically with folks in these conversations and helps guide them in building foundations that lead to specifics. He helps identify the actors (people), the data requiring attention, and the processes that need to be developed. He then builds use cases or descriptions of how these things interact and are acted upon. From there, specific interface specifications may be built and these are wrapped into supporting requirements documentation consistent with the methodologies employed by the company. This simply means the kind of document template holding requirements can vary from the common table napkin to an encyclopedia table of contents and the solution architect follows his company's guidelines.

The outputs created as a result of these conversations can be used to generate level of effort quotes in hours to support client billing and as a baseline in the creation of even more-technical requirements documents and quality assurance test plans. Companies also make use of solution architects when responding to RFPs. An RFP is a Request For Proposal from an organization that wants something built. The solution architect works with his internal company team to create an understanding of what is needed and from that he creates enough documentation to help the company bid on a potential new project.

Being a solution architect can be a lot of fun because you are on the leading edge of what the company is trying to do, you're exposed to new technologies, you're always meeting new people and developing friendships, and you're like a medieval knight protecting the frontiers of the kingdom. When one becomes more senior in his career and isn't interested in a vice president kind of role, being a solution architect can be a nice sweet spot. Or if a person is interested in a senior management position, this can be a nice stepping stone to get there.

The Technical Lead

The technical lead is a very important position which is at the software engineer or senior software engineer level. Think of this person like you would a team captain in sports. He helps organize the team's development activities, mentors his group, makes final decisions when team members disagree on things, supervises project development from a technical perspective, conducts code reviews, and is his team's last line of defense on ensuring the good quality of deliverables.

He regularly participates in requirements analysis discussions with project managers, helps ensure his team members have the necessary computer hardware, software, and other tools they need to do their jobs and is often the critical interviewer of prospective new hires. Technical leads oftentimes help write annual reviews for their team members as well. It is common for technical leads to make the formal shift to engineering management and much of the time they do have an office of their own.

The Business Project Manager vs The Technical Project Manager

Other than the engineers on your own team and your boss, the people with whom you'll spend the most time will be project managers and generally speaking there are two types; the business project manager and the technical project manager.

Project managers set and maintain project timelines, goals or milestones, gather people, data, and other resources, and generally work to keep things moving along. This is an essential role for larger projects that involve systems used by many people, projects affecting multiple systems, and efforts involving more than one department or company- where lots of coordination is required.

Business project managers generally come from outside the I.T. or software development world. They typically are teamed up with a sales person, attend meetings with clients, help drive the sales process, and gather requirements. Most of them do not have technical backgrounds and need support in translating business requirements into technical requirements.

Formally trained project managers are familiar with an organization called the Project Management Institute or PMI. Founded in 1969, the PMI is the world's leading not-for-profit professional membership association for the project, program and portfolio management. Quoting from their official website, *"PMI advances careers, improves organizational success and further matures the profession of project management through its globally recognized standards, certifications, resources, tools, academic research, publications, professional development courses, and networking opportunities."*

Over the years I have had the pleasure of working with Project Management Professional (PMP) certified folks and have found them to be absolutely top notch. PMP certified project managers are to their craft what software engineers are to software development. They know how to run a project, run meetings, ask the right kinds of questions to discern true project requirements, and they know how to keep their projects on track. Such professionals are typically found in larger organizations that have budgets to support this kind of training or start-up companies where they are stakeholders (part owners).

So that's the good news. The reality of the world is the vast majority of people calling themselves project managers are not professionally trained. And as counterintuitive as this may sound, when you gain solid experience *you will need to diplomatically mentor the newer ones.*

In some organizations you may only work with one project manager at a time. In others you may support multiple projects in parallel and interact with more than one project manager simultaneously.

The Junior Project Manager

Similar to a second lieutenant in the army or ensign in the navy, the junior project manager is possibly the third most dangerous person in any organization- slightly behind the politically appointed senior project manager and an unreliable engineer. If their expectations and participation are not carefully monitored and managed, any of them could torpedo your reputation within an organization.

Junior project managers, trained or not, appear in three varieties. The following perceptions are based on my personal experience. About forty percent of them arrive knowing what they don't know and have the level headedness to approach projects pragmatically and with an earnest interest in coming up to speed. This bunch has a lot of upside potential and they are fun with whom to work.

The next fifty percent of junior project managers are timid and so afraid of making the wrong decision they hesitate in making any decisions at all. *This bunch needs encouragement, friendship, and all your best, one-on-one, confidentially-provided advice.* With the right support, many of them will come out of their shells and become very good at their jobs too.

The first two groups mentioned, generally speaking, also possess the prerequisite character traits essential to being a good leader. These include: integrity, honesty, loyalty, respectfulness, responsibility, humility, compassion, fairness, forgiveness, authenticity, courageousness, generosity, perseverance, politeness, kindness, lovingness, optimism, reliability, conscientiousness, and self-discipline.

Although these have been written about in books and on the web for decades, I invite you to check out a site called *LiveBoldAndBloom.com.* They have an article titled, *"20 Good Character Traits Essential For Happiness"* which really does a nice job of providing detail and describing how one can go about building these good character traits.

Now, about our remaining ten percent of junior project managers- to loosely quote and wrongly twist the thoughts of former U.S. Defense Secretary, Donald Rumsfeld, *they don't know what they don't know and the less they know a particular thing the more-ardently they defend their wrong thinking on it.* This type of person will be easy to recognize. He won't yet have all the information necessary to complete your given project but he'll make sure everyone knows he's in charge and he'll begin commanding people willy-nilly to go off spin their wheels in unproductive ways. I write willy-nilly meaning some of the things being requested will make little or no sense to the more senior people on your project and when someone asks him about it he'll stumble coming up with reasoning.

So how will you survive politically and help guide this type of junior project manager? *With discretion, tact, and diplomacy you give him more information and invite him to consider options.* Please read that last sentence again. I experienced years of pain in order to gift it to you and it can save you politically.

For every project and especially when working with this type of project manager, you should set up a special email folder for your project and archive everything. It's logical to keep an audit trail so the team can have a *lessons learned meeting* when it's all done. In time, you're bound to work with some of these project managers. Most organizations come to recognize the bad ones and through natural selection they are reassigned or let go. Until then you will have to play a little defense with these folks to protect your reputation. And that's just part of life.

The Senior Project Manager

Senior project managers come in two varieties; ones who have worked their way into the position and politically appointed ones- those given the job by a friend. The ones who have earned their way there are truly amazing- they know your company's business, its internal policies and procedures, are very organized, and have a calm and happy demeanor that puts smiles on everyone. When you are the new person, they welcome and mentor you. They proactively reach out to ensure everyone has all the information and tools necessary to complete their tasks. They produce clear process flow diagrams and Gantt charts outlining the project schedule and dependencies. And they are open to innovative ideas in team meetings. You'll really enjoy being involved in their projects and in time begin to realize how much they help you grow professionally and even personally.

The politically appointed senior project manager can be the second most dangerous person in an organization. Here and there you'll find a qualified one but more often than not the *friend-appointee* is a train wreck waiting to happen. The challenge with them is they utilize their friendship with a higher-up in your organization to cover for blunders. And if that friendship is really strong the higher-up instrumental in getting his friend the position won't take lightly your highlighting the person's mistakes; at least for a while. So how do you handle this scenario?

The first step is to recognize and respect that relationship. See the bigger picture of what's going on here and don't do anything stupid to trigger it. The second step is to learn the art of diplomacy and the tactic of deflecting direct character and intellectual assaults levied by these Atilla-The-Hun or clueless buffoon appointees. The political appointee's relationship with the higher-up and other personal relationships between your coworkers are reasons your development of tact and discretion when trying to nudge people in the right direction is so important. *The goal is to achieve your objectives with the minimum amount of conflict or no conflict at all. You do this by privately inviting him to look at the plusses and minuses of proceeding one way or another and then by asking him his thoughts- either in person or in a one-on-one email.*

When you take this approach, eight times out of ten he will come to the same conclusion you did. Those last two times he will let you in on some information you didn't have which will explain his reasoning for going in a different direction. And you know what? *It's all good.*

This is especially true with managers to whom you directly report. We each play a role in a project. As the engineer, tempting as it may seem your job isn't to make the final decision on things. *Your job is to provide your manager with the best information available so he can make the decision.* When you do that, he'll come back to you for advice as his go-to engineer. You see, it's not about him being right or you being right. *It's about what's right for the project- and the manager is the final arbiter of that.*

Software Engineering Manager

The special job of managing engineers or as my friends and I like to call it "trying to herd cats," is that of the engineering manager. The vast majority of the time this manager was himself at one time an accomplished engineer. And as with a few of the other positions described, you'll find some make the transition from engineer to engineering manager smoothly and some do not.

A few times in my career I had the distinction of serving in this role. For a year stretch I supervised seventeen java developers and five database developers. And more recently over a five year stretch I managed a great bunch of software and database engineers ranging from a team of eight to twenty-six in number. The job of an engineering manager is very different from that of a project manager or a software engineer. The project manager is in charge of just a given project. The engineers assigned to his project report to him for that project, however, they may be working multiple projects in parallel. The software engineer may lead, write software, and even mentor, but at the end of the day he isn't the one making command decisions.

The engineering manager is responsible for creating the environment necessary for his team to be successful. These things include, but aren't limited to:

- Hiring and building his team.

- Selecting the technical leads within it.

- Establishing productive business relationships with everyone outside of his department.

- Authoring or approving, maintaining, and training his team on procedures for the full lifecycle of software development activities.

- Negotiating with the information technology (I.T.) manager for his team's laptops, software, peripherals, internal and external servers and disk space, and other computer related supplies.

- Helping to decide whether a piece of hardware or software is project-specific and billable to a particular client, or a capital expenditure which is funded from a separate bucket of accounting money designated for items useful to many clients over time.

- Speaking with project managers to help them understand the process and procedures associated with requesting resources for projects, reviewing their project documents and highlighting areas needing refinement prior to project kick off.

- Touching base with the various teams under him as their projects evolve.

- Should a project go a little off course in scope or schedule, he consults with the project manager and mentors team members as needed. Having usually a good ten years of experience, he's been through similar trials and tribulations and sees these challenges as little speed bumps- things that can be worked through.

In the recent five year stretch as an engineering manager I found it to be the most interesting yet energy sapping of all my experiences. One hundred to one hundred fifty emails per day, non-stop meetings, and night and weekend work were very common. That engineering manager position was for a pharmaceutical marketing company- a line of business that is extremely fast-paced.

It is also common for the engineering manager to give presentations to project managers, senior management, and sometimes even clients. He is the voice of the engineering team and in Star Trek The Next Generation parlance, he is Geordi La Forge.

I.T. Manager

The information technology (I.T.) manager supervises the teams of people responsible for providing an organization's help desk; software; network connectivity; email; web, database, file, and print servers; printers; telecommunications; desktop and laptop computers, PDAs; and other services. And he also provides inputs to the Chief Information Office on data security. It's a big responsibility. Most often this person has a bachelor's or master's degree in information systems, however, those with a degree in computer science sometimes take on this challenge as well.

There are technical aspects to this position but the best I.T. managers are very skilled diplomats. Providing the aforementioned products and services is a delicate balancing act involving department and company budgets and negotiating with groups competing for resources. I.T. managers also help develop policy and supervise company training with respect to the use of the company's information technology. They regularly meet with and present to senior management and they work with the company chief information officer (CIO) in developing longer term strategies.

Because of how closely together they work, the I.T. manager is oftentimes the software engineering manager's best friend. Responsibility for the proper use of the company's assets, especially its servers, falls to the I.T. manager. Therefore, it's incumbent upon the software engineering manager to convince him through conversation and example that his department has put proper protocols in place and conducts solid training to have earned the I.T. manager's trust. This takes time. However once the software engineering manager has earned that trust, work life is so much easier.

Agile Teams

The widely held definition of *agile software development* is that it describes a set of values and principles for software development under which requirements and solutions evolve through the collaborative effort of self-organizing cross-functional teams. It advocates adaptive planning, evolutionary development, early delivery, continuous improvement, and it encourages rapid and flexible response to change.

This is very different than the development method known as *waterfall*- where requirements are determined up front and there is one straight-line path to building, testing, and delivering a software product. Agile development thoughtfully organizes the types of technology professionals I've described into specific roles they play throughout a cyclical software development, testing, and delivery process.

At the time of this writing *Amazon.com* has listed for sale, 1,142 books covering agile project management. What's important for you to know while exploring your interest in software development is that agile is the next step in the evolution of professional software development and worthy of further study once you understand the basics. To read a good overview of agile, I invite you to check out the website *ScrumAlliance.org.*

CIO – The Higher You Rise, The More You Have To Care About Politics

The chief information officer (CIO) always exists in larger organizations and sometimes even in smaller ones. He usually has both the software engineering department and information technology department under him. Beyond the overall responsibility for those departments, his job is to provide advice and assistance to senior managers on I.T. acquisition and management and to develop, maintain, and ensure implementation of a sound and integrated I.T. architecture. He mentors I.T. and software engineering managers and also provides high-level, company-wide guidance on one of the company's most valuable assets: its data. That is, how data comes in, where it's stored, who sees it, how it's packaged for internal or external use, and its final disposition.

This executive-level position as well as any other requires a combination of supervisory experience and great diplomacy skills. And, yes, the *big guy* has a nice office.

The H.R. Manager

There are lots of sites on the web where you can learn about managerial positions. At the time of this writing, *Monster.com* for example describes the human resources (H.R.) manager position generally in fourteen, long-winded, paragraphs. Let's look at the relationship between H.R. managers and the engineering department more specifically.

H.R. helps recruit new engineers. The engineering manager provides the H.R. department with position titles, job descriptions, and lists of technical and personal skills needed. These write ups are usually saved as a templates for future openings and they evolve over time with the company's needs. In most companies jobs are posted internally first- giving existing employees the opportunity to apply for an upward or even lateral, cross-departmental move. If an internal candidate hasn't been found, after usually two to four weeks, H.R. will post positions externally on the most popular techie job websites. And each company has its preferred sites, often driven by the type of position. For executive and difficult to fill, more-senior technical positions, it's common for H.R. teams to make use of executive and technical recruiters.

The H.R. team handles many other things as well. These include, yet aren't limited to:

- Scheduling and managing the interview process.

- New hire and current employee payroll and benefits paperwork and ongoing support in those areas.

- Providing and supporting company training.

- The formalities of employee discipline, firings, and promotions

- Organizing larger company social events.

H.R. personnel are trained to know employment laws and in my experience offer good advice in handling situations with co-workers that might be challenging. This having been written, it's best to work discretely with your direct boss on things before going to H.R.

Look at the company as one big machine with a lot of moving parts. The job of the human resources department is to help ensure things run legally and smoothly.

Sales People

People who sell things exist virtually everywhere in life. In fact, a fun thing to try sometime is to look at how many things you can see with your eyes where some type of salesmanship or marketing isn't happening. In America, you'll go about five seconds before bumping into some kind of commercial. And that's not a bad thing when you view it from the perspective that these are people with a solution trying to find the people with a need.

Your company's sales team interacts directly with clients. They form business relationships and even personal friendships with them to earn their trust and their business. Good sales people know their product line inside and out and the really good ones are adept at identifying underlying or unspoken requirements too. Just as with junior project managers, you may someday have the opportunity to help guide and mentor junior sales people. Of course there are senior sales people and project managers with this direct responsibility, however, their technical backgrounds are limited so you helping them gain some high-level technical insights is usually appreciated. Care must be taken though not to drag them too far out into the weeds when describing technical things.

Successful sales people with whom I've worked have been work-hard, play-hard, "Type A" personality folks. Because they are the lifeblood of the organization, getting client contracts that generate revenue, they oftentimes also garner special treatment in the form of fancy, company-paid dinners, parties, and weekend retreats. Most companies for whom I've worked try to keep these activities on the quiet side but sooner or later you'll come to learn of them. And you know what? *For the revenue they generate these nice little perks are truly earned and I've got nothing but love for the sales team.*

Most companies have a senior vice president of sales reporting directly to the chief executive officer (CEO). This person provides guidance to the sales people on his team and participates in senior-level strategy formulation.

As you become a more experienced engineer, you will have the opportunity to work with and gain the respect of your sales team. In time they will come directly to you for your thoughts on the products your company offers and even technical advice on how to present them. And that respect for your expertise can give an engineer a really great feeling.

Senior Management

So what is senior management? This is the core team of most experienced company executives and they provide strategic advice and guidance to help run the company. For the uninitiated, there are generally two types of activities: tactical and strategic.

Tactical activities are the things on which junior and mid-level people focus most. They are discrete actions tied to a specific project or task. Researching requirements, authoring a class of properties and methods for a specific website, designing a database, and writing a training manual are all examples of tactical activities. Strategic activities are at a much higher level. Examples of strategic activities would be, say, deciding to lease a building for five years due to business growth or to conclude it would be a good policy to permit productive software engineers to work from home a few days a week. Of course, these are just examples. Most senior management teams have usually seen and done pretty much everything a company could encounter. If your company is doing well then your senior management team has learned how to guide, when to get more involved, and when to step back and let great people like you do your thing.

Senior management folks are like politicians in the real world- you see them at important events like the company holiday party, announcements of big corporate initiatives, and company all-hands meetings a few times per year. The rest of the time they are mentoring your company's vice presidents and strategizing. From the perspective of the average employee this may not seem like much, but trust me they spend a lot of time thinking things through and oftentimes the little policy shifts and slightly new directions in which your company turns can result in big differences. Sometimes those differences are immediately noticeable and sometimes they take many months or more before effects are seen. It's important to give them the benefit of the doubt, support their initiatives, and see how things play out.

At the company holiday party you will get to meet them and even get to chat for a few minutes. That's a great time to become acquainted. Company websites oftentimes have a page with profiles of senior management; their years of experience, colleges they attended, what they studied, and more. You may find their backgrounds interesting and good small talk kibble.

Clients

Clients are the companies and people who pay your company money for the goods and services you provide. The smaller your company, the more likely it is you will meet them and sometimes even service them directly. *When you are talking with them, you are the face of your company.* Their experience with you will have influence on whether or not they will continue to do business with your company. No pressure there, right?

Actually there's no need for nervousness when interfacing with a client. Early on in your career, client meetings will include more senior people of your company and you can defer to them on how the meetings will go- just let them drive. As you gain experience you will become more comfortable with your clients and in working with them more directly. Soon enough, you will enter these meetings with a big smile, great confidence, and conveying such sincere interest in their satisfaction they'll find it hard to resist your ideas.

Think back to when you were a freshman in high school. You were a little nervous those first few days, weren't you? We all were. Now think about your first week as a senior in high school. You feel and walk like you own the place because you are comfortable; you've fully acclimated. It's the exact same thing in business.

Technical Recruiters

Technical recruiters are companies and people that specialize in locating high-caliber people with unique skill sets. And they do it for a fee; oftentimes for an amount equal to a percentage of the person's first year salary. For example, when I was hired in 2006 I learned the company finding me made $8,000 or eight percent of my first year salary. I received the full $100,000. They were paid a separate eight percent fee.

From an engineer's perspective, once you have a few years of experience a technical recruiter will happily help find you a new position. The process is pretty straight forward too. You just walk in to meet them or call them on the phone, fill out some forms, provide a resume or point them to your LinkedIn profile, and chat. They have senior engineers on staff who will conduct a technical interview with you. Much of the time they will ask you to take a short test to demonstrate your knowledge.

If you do well on the test, they'll immediately want to work with you. And yes, they too like Curve Breakers– those who can do well on their tests.

PART VI: CHOOSING YOUR FIRST COMPANY

Yes, You Get To Choose

One of the many wonderful things for which our American forefathers fought was life, liberty, and the pursuit of happiness. *Those freedoms are broad ranging and come with your accepting responsibility for the result of your life choices.* And the selection of an initial company isn't a final one- it's not like you get a single shot at it. Over the years I've worked for more than twenty companies; by choice. Some of your decisions will work out well and some won't. That's just the way the cookie crumbles. The good news is should you wish or need, you can change course and prepare to move in a new direction virtually anytime you like. There are a number of personal preferences in deciding the first organization for which you'll work. Beyond the type of work the company does, these include but are not limited to: company size, geographical location, the company's willingness to support you in relocating, housing affordability, and government vs. private sector work. Let's take a dive into these and I'll reveal what I've learned.

Intellectual Challenge

Have you ever taken a moment just to people-watch others doing their jobs? Some jobs require coordination of multiple activities that keep one's brain monotonously firing on all cylinders while not actually changing gears. For example, a developer on a big government maintenance contract responsible for running reports and making minor configuration file changes isn't stretching himself intellectually nor maximizing his potential. There aren't a lot of tough puzzles to solve there and that kind of job eventually gets automated out of existence. A side effect of the absolutely boring day-to-day drudgery of this kind of job is that the leading-edge skill set of the developer doing it begins to fade over time. Some people accept this kind of existence but I never could. It's a shameful disservice to the hard work one puts in to becoming a professional engineer.

On the other hand, developers involved in creating new products or custom solutions have some great tools at their disposal and tons of ways to utilize them. And the environments in which their end products must run often vary; making the challenge even more interesting. *The kind of job less likely to be automated and more likely to keep you intellectually stimulated is one where much of how you are going to solve a puzzle isn't written down, where you continuously need to research things and make tactical decisions.* For junior engineers, this is where the fun really begins.

If you've worked hard and completed courses in calculus, statistics, data structures, theory of algorithms, data communications, operating systems, compiler construction, and more then you are up for some next level computer science. If you've done all these things then let me tell you, the world is desperately seeking your talent to help chart new frontiers in every field. *Don't be shy.*

Does The Work Matter?

Each of us has a core set of values and principles- a foundation of things that really matter to us. And at the end of the day we need to be able to look ourselves in the mirror and say, "I'm comfortable this place is worthy of my time." So when you are considering whether or not to apply to a company, look to see if their activities make a positive difference in the kind of world in which you want to live. Will your working there genuinely help other people, our country, perhaps the entire world, or are they just making and selling common stuff? Can you mentally sell yourself on their mission?

It's understandable for people fresh out of school, especially those who've been living on a steady diet of cheap ramen noodles, to go for the first good-paying position they find. They then climb into a bunch of consumer debt- using credit cards to buy a bunch of junk- realize they've chosen a company adding no social value whatsoever, and then feel stuck there. So consider positions in their entirety. Companies are more than places to earn salaries and benefits. We feel the most career satisfaction when we are doing interesting things that matter to us- that we are making a difference in the service of causes much larger than ourselves.

Given the vast number of engineering jobs and your in-demand skill set, you will be in a great position to choose. Consider also the perfect fit of a company, a particular company you really like, might not have an opening at that moment.

However, there may be a directly related company that does. Let's say, for example, a new engineer is interested in supporting scientific research into cures of child illnesses. She might apply to pharmaceutical companies doing research in this area. However, she might also apply to children's hospitals. Similar line of work, similar cause, and the experience there could help one land a clinical research position in a year or two. Get the idea?

Additionally, not all people who major in computer science or a closely-related degree end up programming. In fact, there are many who instead choose to become business analysts, systems analysts, or junior project managers upon graduation and never write a line of code. People in these roles benefit greatly from the analytical skills one builds in earning a degree in engineering. So this is your formal invitation to take a deep breath, smile, and look at the job market as a big box of freshly-opened treats where you get to make an informed choice. This will be one of the most fun times in your life. Enjoy!

Large vs. Small

Companies come in all shapes and sizes. Some have only one location and distribute their products from their headquarters. Others have a headquarters with smaller locations across the country. And still others are large with regional distribution centers and locations worldwide. The role you play both initially and down the line will vary with the size of the company.

- Where You End Up When You Start

    In very large companies, the entry level engineer is typically assigned to a group with a very specific task. The task might be directly tied to manufacturing, finance, or maintenance of an existing contract for example. There might be dozens of similar groups like this one in other locations. There is a bit of safety in an assignment like this because more senior people are available to help guide you and in most cases you can more comfortably acclimate without a lot of pressure. Big companies also have well-formed support teams such as an information technology (I.T.) team already supporting hundreds if not thousands of people. Therefore they are likely prepared for most any contingency and have most everything you need in stock. Companies of size also usually have a cafeteria with good deals on lunch and are even sometimes open for breakfast.

One downside in big companies is strategic decisions you don't understand will just kind of happen For example, their decision to relocate the manufacturing of product A to the city of Cleveland will be announced with no explanation. And many times your boss won't know or if he does he won't have permission to tell you the reasoning behind it. Sometimes decisions like that are made simply to be more efficient. Sometimes it's because they have a plan to close down your location and they cannot afford to have employees bail to a new job before they complete the plan. Either way, it may not be immediately clear.

In very small companies, it's common for the entry level engineer to support almost everything the company does. Smaller companies are fighting to stay in business and the engineer plays a critical role in helping them survive. In this environment, one can gain a wide range of valuable experience in a short amount of time.

Support departments such as I.T. are small and they have to special order basic things such as laptops and software. Smaller companies rarely have a cafeteria so lunch will be something you bring with you or you'll go out to eat. Going out for lunch can be great fun and a nice way to get to know people. Also, your fellow coworkers will know the best places to go for a low-cost lunch and in many urban areas there are lunch buffets. When I worked in Reston, Virginia we nicknamed them "feed bags." We knew an Italian one, a Mexican one, and a Chinese one and we'd alternate. When you first start working you'll experience the joy of earning a paycheck and actually living a little. *That having been written, it's a good idea to write down what you are spending on lunches and track it. At the end of the week or month total it all up and then look at your budget to decide what works for you.* We didn't go all the time, maybe twice a week and it was good team bonding time.

In the smaller company, business decisions are made quickly and the client asking for help the loudest gets the most attention. There may be one or two more senior engineers already on staff and their opinion of the seemingly chaotic state of the company will be worth noting. One upside to working with a smaller company is you will have opportunity to meet everyone working there from the company president on down. And you will oftentimes be in the loop with respect to why decisions are made.

- Company-Paid Training Budget

Many companies support or even require their employees stay up to speed with the latest software and other business development tools. Additional, non-technical training is also deemed necessary in many cases. This training may be in effective communications, negotiating, and eventually managerial training. It has been a common practice, especially for engineers, that companies fund formal training such as graduate school. And they sometimes bring instructors on-site to provide more-specific training. Graduate school and other classes are usually paid as a reimbursement after the course ends. For example, I've seen one hundred percent (100%) paid for an "A" grade, seventy-five percent (75%) paid for a "B" grade, and nothing paid for a "C" grade or below. This kind of formula serves as a very good incentive as graduate school can be an expensive proposition.

A short bit of advice, if you are working full time and considering graduate school start with just one course. Get comfortable with the work, night school, and life balance. After the first course you can evaluate whether or not you want to try two courses at once. If you have little to no social life you might be able to pull off taking two courses- but it's a real challenge.

It's also common for companies to require employees sign a contract to stay with them for a certain number of years in return for paying for graduate school. Companies want to benefit from the employee's enhanced knowledge and abilities. It's a fair trade.

Towards the end of the typical job interview, if you can sense it is going well, ask about training. However, this should be done diplomatically. For example a good way to ask would be, "With your company's great reputation, I'm wondering what kind of formal training your employees take? Does the company have a program for continuing education?" They'll either convey the information or invite you to ask HR about it.

- The Term "Start Up"

The term "Start Up" is a fascinating one. There's the definition of it and then there's how it usually translates to the work environment. The term identifies a company that is kind of new or is just getting going. So let's think about that for a second. Just getting going can also mean they've been around a while yet don't have a lot of clients or may not be generating much revenue.

How does this translate to the work environment? Well, in the late 1990's there was a period called the ".Com Boom." From, say, 1996 through 2002 or so start-ups were popping up everywhere. *In some ways it was an engineer's dream, in other ways it was an engineer's nightmare.* These newer companies used funding from their founders or from venture capitalists to get the business up and running. However, getting a company going requires parallel execution in multiple areas. These companies were trying to get sales, project management, I.T., development and manufacturing, H.R. and more all going at the same time. It required everyone to put in lots of overtime, oftentimes crazy amounts of hours, for their base pay (no overtime pay) and the promise of a bright future. Sometimes a company offered the promise of shares that would have value only if it went public. The vast majority of the time these companies never generated enough revenue to go big-time. For every one that became super successful, there were a thousand companies that burned through their venture capital then collapsed into a heap of ashes.

As you gain experience you will make professional friends and opportunities to work with start-ups may present themselves. You'll need to evaluate the proposition at the time and ask: How large is their market? How good is their product? What is their ability to gain traction or get people to use their product? Are their sales and marketing teams flexible in cutting deals to get clients?

This is called "vetting"- you will be evaluating their idea; looking at the pros and cons. It can help to write them down on paper, side by side. Then you will be able to decide whether or not you think it's worth your time to help the start-up with passion.

The last bit of advice I'll give on start-ups here is this- if a recruiter, the marketing bunch, or some rando-craigslist-computer-gig dude excitedly says, "There's a potential client base of ten million users! Just think if we get even one percent of that!"- *don't be fooled by it. Ask to see specifically how the company is going to get its first ten clients.* Lots of people fall for the one percent calculation without a specific plan for getting even the first few. I was burned with this hype at least twice myself where I worked more than a thousand hours for a startup that burned through its capital and then simply folded; unable to attract paying clients. Watch out for it.

• Opportunities From That Position

Another key factor in choosing a company is the kind of next-level opportunities the starting position will offer. Those can vary by size of company, growth it is experiencing, location, and other criteria. As an entry level engineer in a *very large company* it's common to be assigned to a group focused on a single area or project and to be there for a couple of years or more. The upside to this is you'll learn the company's best practices and become comfortable with that kind of structured environment. Another upside is you'll soon be able to list that large, well-known company on your resume. And that does have value down the road. The downside to starting in a very large company is you'll be a very small fish in a very big pond. By that I mean you likely won't get a lot of facetime with upper management and opportunities for them to see you shine will be limited. So there are pros and cons.

As an entry level engineer in a *small company* it's often the case they are short-handed. Small companies look for people to jump in and help wherever they can. And that represents opportunity to play many roles and get noticed. Your sweat equity will pay dividends down the line and that's a pretty big plus. The downside to smaller companies is they aren't well known so their name on your resume won't be recognizable. Additionally, small companies are super busy and act quickly in everything they do. In college you are taught some basic engineering steps such as using process flow and project planning tools. Smaller companies oftentimes don't have the nicer tools and you may have to fly by the seat of your pants using spreadsheets and text documents. And that can lead to cutting corners and other bad habits unacceptable in larger, more professional organizations.

In what they used to call "olden times," employees would often spend their entire careers with a single company. Then in the 1980's I began to notice that companies were publicly stating their decisions to open and close locations, to make or cease making certain products, and by extension to keep or eliminate departments or divisions *were based on satisfying stock holder desires to see a profit.* It wasn't that this was something new, only that my eyes were finally open to it. Stock holders provide the company with money it can use to do lots of things and in exchange the company is expected to increase stock value or pay dividends. This means publicly traded companies and ones which took money from investors are more committed to them and lesser so to their employees.

So, what were employees of these kinds of companies to do? Some unionized to protect jobs, wages, and benefits. And highly-skilled or in high demand employees had their eyes opened to the fact loyalty is a two-way street- that they were and are free to act in their own best interest.

Now to leap ahead a bit, at some point in your time with every company you are going to reach a crossroads- the realization that you have maximized your upside within a position and it's time to make a move. If you find yourself under a boss who has established a set of low standards with respect to the challenges you can take on or a manager who doesn't trust you to try to take things to the next level, you have four options. First, you could settle for this boring existence- something I would never recommend. Second you could invest the time to change the mindset of your boss- but this can be tough if he is firmly ensconced in what he thinks is a "safe space." Third, you could try to make a lateral move to another department. And lastly, you can move on to a new company or even create one of your own.

If the choice becomes to move, it's important to first *quietly* do a personal inventory of your skills and project experience. You'll likely have many new things to add to your resume or LinkedIn profile and those items will help you get into more interesting or challenging work at greater pay.

Big City vs. Out In The Country

When close to graduation, most students have a pretty good idea whether they want to begin their career working in the city or in the country. And younger people, full of energy, tend to gravitate towards cities with their many museums, concert venues, exotic restaurants, people from all over the world, and fun activities. However, later in their careers many people come to appreciate the quality of a slower pace of life. So let's talk about the upsides and downsides of the city and country.

The upside of starting one's career in the big city is that cities are full of companies and opportunities. In the first few years of your career you will acquire many skills not taught in the typical engineering college curriculum. And after two to three years, having those skills make you much more valuable in the marketplace. At that point you'll have to decide whether to stay or to jump to a new company. Within your company there may be opportunities to grow through continued education at the graduate level or chances to take on technical lead responsibilities. Conversely, you could take those new skills to another company that needs them and is willing to give you a nice pay raise.

Now if your company is out in the country, the likelihood is good there won't be that many other companies in the area competing to hire you. Out in the country means everything is spread out, and there just aren't as many people. There may be a few companies but oftentimes their officers know each other, perhaps through the local country club, and they prefer to avoid bidding wars for talent. They know employees don't have a lot of local options and gamble they aren't going to up and leave. For inexperienced employees with few options or even senior ones who have put down roots by buying a house, out-in-the-country becomes a take this job or leave it proposition.

In the big city there are so many companies it's almost impossible for them to collude in keeping salaries and benefits down. As a scarce resource, engineers are in a great position to take control of their own destiny. Put simply, you can easily move to a new company anytime you like. Now I'm not advocating jumping every six months or even year because it could denote instability or an unwillingness to persist through challenging work situations.

Early in one's career the excitement of the big city is certainly alluring. It's a much faster pace of life and the idea of living in an apartment with a roommate or two sounds just fine. In fact your vision or what you see will be limited to the things directly in front of you. The further along you progress in your career and older you get, the broader that view will become. After a year or three, it's natural you'll come to feel you don't want a roommate but rather a romantic interest with whom to build a future. And then you may realize you want a life where you aren't a tiny fish in a very big, super-busy, polluted, traffic and human-laden, crime-infested, metropolitan pond.

Now this isn't to say one cannot create a small oasis in the middle of the concrete jungle; many people do. Some of the finest examples I've seen of this are in New Orleans, Louisiana. Google "French Quarter Courtyards," click the Pinterest link, and you'll see what I mean. Simple yet smart architectural tricks have been used for centuries to create beautiful, hidden escapes right in the middle of large cities. But these are the exception and not the rule.

In the big city there's a good chance you can utilize public transportation or similar means to get around. Out in the country you're going to need a car, auto insurance, gas money, and to spend money regularly maintaining it. Also, generally speaking, living in the city will have some overhead costs not prevalent out in the country. One of these is taxes. In my area for example, Philadelphia has a city wage tax of 3.92% that comes right out of your check. That's in addition to all the other taxes one pays. The city does, however, provide cultural and other niceties such as museums and activities we don't have out in the suburbs. So here too there's a trade-off.

There are two vectors here running in parallel. One is your personal definition of happiness; who you are and the way you live. That will evolve throughout your life and is a very personal, subjective concept. The other is your career- what you can do immediately after graduation to get on a good track. And for this one I do have a specific thought.

Recommendation: For the first four to six years migrate to a large city and take a position with a big, well known corporation. The training you will receive there will help you build upon the foundation you started in college. You'll see how large companies operate and this will reinforce your desire to act as a professional engineer. At the end of that time, you'll also have the name of a respected company on your resume and be positioned for the next great opportunity whether it's within that company or another one that would love to leverage the upgraded You v2.0.

Company Paid Moves

The law of supply and demand drives the American business world. If a much-needed resource is in limited supply, companies will make the extra effort to obtain it. This is as true with personnel as it is with high-end software. Over the years I've seen companies put people up in fancy hotels, pay them per diem (daily money for expenses such as food and having their laundry done), offer extended car rentals or reimbursement for mileage, and more. And I've experienced it myself on multiple occasions.

Early in my post-college career I accepted employment with a defense company called E-Systems, later acquired by Raytheon, located more than two hundred miles from my home. The position required a top secret security clearance and solid software development skills. Fortunately, my years as a cryptologic technician in the navy and my freshly-minted degree in computer science made me the rare commodity they wanted.

The salary and vacation offer they made was gracious and they were willing to pay for the move. For up to two months they were willing to house my family and me in a nice hotel room with a living room and kitchenette. While there, they also paid my full salary, seventy-five dollars per day per diem, and paid the moving and storage of all our household items until we found our own place. After six weeks in the hotel, I found a nice townhouse and we moved. However, if it weren't for the company's offer I would have never been able to afford the move. I'm very grateful they were so generous.

This was a real world illustration of the law of supply and demand. Would the company have made these accommodations for a secretary or a maintenance person? No. Not for lack of human compassion or because these roles don't help the organization but because those positions are easier to fill. It is a lot harder to find an academic curve-breaking engineer with a naval security background. If you're good, you'll also find this to be true as you progress through your career. Senior engineers and managers garner this kind of special attention too. The good ones are hard to find and companies respect that.

This having been written, each company's needs are unique. Some offer company-paid moves and some do not. The only way to know is to ask. However, when to ask is important. In the interview preparation section below I discuss the art of the deal.

Buying A Home And Establishing Credit

As you work your way through high school and college it's perfectly normal to daydream now about where and how you might like to live. And it's also normal to think of buying a home. While I am not a financial advisor, I can write to some of the factors you'll want to consider when making the decision. Just as you would carefully consider the full lifecycle of an important project before embarking upon it, you'll want to do the same thing when considering buying a home. Note I wrote, "home," and not "house." A house is an object or location while a home is where you truly live.

Fresh out of college and just into your first job you could obtain a house but in order to make that a home you'll want to add some things many college kids overlook. For example, you might want to have furniture, dishes, silverware, towels,

By Tom Nicholas

bed linens, drapes, and, well, now you get the picture. Getting the home loan itself could be a challenge. Unless you have a Veteran's Administration (VA) guarantee, lenders like to see a decent credit rating and employment stability. The first four to six years of an engineering career is when many people experience rapid professional growth; from entry level programmer, to developer, to senior developer or even technical lead. In that time people often move to other companies and see their salaries grow significantly.

Over a ten year period I watched two of my single guy friends work a financial plan perfectly. They had graduated from the University of Virginia with STEM degrees. Both took great positions with well-known companies. They lived in a good Northern Virginia neighborhood where a two bedroom apartment went for about $1,200 per month. Each was making more than $75,000 per year and after a while much more. Yet they split the rent, stashed away money, and still enjoyed fabulous personal lives- making friends, dating, driving reasonably decent cars, and taking the occasional vacation. After about ten years they were in their thirties, income nearly doubled from the above, and were ready to settle down, buy a home, and get married. They were patient and it really worked well for them both.

Think about it, until you experience living out on your own as an adult in a big city, the suburbs, or the country you aren't going to really know which locale you prefer. And drawing these conclusions based upon your own experience is an important part of life.

When you move out on your own you're going to need or want some things for which you don't have the cash. At that point you'll likely apply for a credit card. Credit cards allow you to buy things over time. In exchange for that privilege, you pay an extra percentage or loan rate above the cost of the items you are buying. With no history of taking out and paying back loans, your first card might not have that great a loan rate. Over time as you pay things off your credit rating will go up, and loan companies will notice your responsible behavior and begin to compete for your business- pitching you credit offers via mail, email, and even via social media.

So what is a *Credit Rating?* A credit rating is a numerical evaluation of your trustworthiness in paying back loans. Lenders report your loan and payment activity to the three major credit reporting agencies; Equifax, Experian, and Trans Union. These agencies provide reports to consumers and lenders alike; detailing your creditworthiness. These reports help lenders determine the risk in lending to you. And that risk is what they use to set your loan rate. Here are some credit tips:

- Every time you move to a new location, be sure to fill out an address change card at your old post office telling them to forward your mail.

- Contact all three credit reporting agencies to tell them your new address. Credit card companies oftentimes get your address from the reporting agencies. This will reduce the likelihood of third-party companies sending free offers to your old address. Identity thieves have been known to steal mail of someone who has moved and illegally obtain credit cards in his name. When they buy items in your name you could get stuck with the bill. *You must be diligent in protecting your personal data.*

- Be careful when building your credit to set aside some money into a savings account. Although engineers are very employable, markets and companies change and it's not always clear when you might have to make a jump to a new company.

- With respect to learning about money management, mastering credit and debt, and planning ahead, I recommend checking out the website *FeedThePig.org.*

Recommendation: After moving to a big city and taking a position with a large organization, get or share an apartment with one or more responsible roommates. Once you are settled, begin setting aside money for a home and the things you'll want in it. This step could take a few years. Meanwhile, smile and enjoy life. You will have earned it!

Government vs. Private Sector

Working for the government, be it at the state or federal level, is very different than working in the private sector. And not all government agencies are created equally. This having been written, each has certain characteristics or things for which they are known.

Most but not all government agencies have the reputation of offering lower base pay than private sector companies, more valuable and flexible benefits, and the majority of the time are clogged with more than enough burdensome engineering practices and red tape to demotivate the most positive, energetic person. However, that bureaucracy oftentimes provides job security. Yes this is nonsensical and inefficient. And yes, it has been my experience it's true.

Scientists and many non-technical professionals thrive in such well-ordered environments. In no particular order, the Los Alamos National Lab, the Defense Advanced Research Project Agency (DARPA, with whom I worked as a contractor), the Nuclear Regulatory Commission, the Government Accountability Office (GAO), the National Aeronautics And Space Administration (NASA), the Intelligence Community (NSA, CIA, FBI), the Department Of State, Department Of Justice, and others do some fascinating and interesting work with big upsides for the United States of America and humanity in general.

A few large-sized private sector companies and almost all mid-sized and smaller ones have a very different reputation. They or their senior management teams are in a yearly or quarterly fight for their existence- something dependent upon the real and tangible flow of cash coming in via sales and money flowing out due to expenditures such as cost of goods, salaries, insurance, rent, taxes, and much more. *These companies are in tough competition for engineering talent and usually provide excellent compensation and decent benefits in exchange for longer work hours and less job security.* They experience the pains of organizational growth and shrinkage tied to their sales numbers and it's common for them to make and then break their own rules and policies to meet customer needs.

This kind of chaos is oftentimes embraced by go-get-em, "Type A" personality people, however, it has side effects. While it creates seemingly endless career opportunities it can also burn a person out and put tremendous strain on one's non-work, personal relationships. So what do I mean by that?

Several years back I was compelled to work twelve and a half hours on a Saturday because one of our partner companies pushed a web service into production that wasn't fully regression tested. It failed on a Friday evening so, as we used to say in the navy, "all hands were on deck" until the issue was resolved. As a salaried employee we didn't get overtime for extra hours. Additionally, my wife and I bought expensive tickets to an anniversary event she was super-excited to attend and we were more than an hour late getting to it so I ended up in her dog house. There will be times in your career you'll have to choose between supporting your organization's needs and standing by your personal or family commitments. The best advice I can offer is to talk it over with those involved, think long term, and choose carefully.

To this point I've discussed the government and private sector as two separate types of work. As a regular course of business though, they also work together. Government agencies have charters to do certain kinds of work for which they either aren't fully staffed or lack the expertise. So they contract things out to private companies and act as supervisors to ensure the work is done well.

For example, in the year 2000 I was running a private software development consulting company called Tommyland Corporation. We had only two employees and Tommyland subcontracted with the Reston, Virginia office of Titan Corporation. Titan had a larger contract with The Federal Aviation Administration (FAA) to help them track the several billions of dollars in federal funds given annually to large and small airports nationwide.

Each year the FAA provides to the United States Congress a report detailing how the money is being used. With over two thousand airports buying equipment, doing maintenance, and engaging in multi-year improvement efforts, tracking it is a major effort. Every dollar utilized for radar upgrades at major airports like Atlanta Hartsfield and Chicago O'Hare to every penny put towards buttressing runways at tiny airports like the one in Atka, Alaska is in this report.

Altogether there were thirteen of us on this four plus million dollar annual contract. Some were software developers, some database developers, and some data analysts. Private sector companies like Titan do everything they can to put forth their best efforts. This helps protect their relationship with the government agency- the source of the revenue stream. Likewise, government agencies prefer working with known commodities; companies that have the reputation for delivering the goods. The challenge for the government comes in acting in the best interests of United States taxpayers. Efficient use of taxpayer dollars is the best result for the least amount of money. To that end, the government has enacted law for competition in federal contracting. And in my multiple government contract experiences, including the Titan one, they were very good about following it.

So as you can see, there are pros and cons in working for either type of organization; private and governmental. And most of the time to the benefit of citizens and the nation as a whole, they regularly work together.

Interview Preparation

When you ask the average person what he does to prepare for an interview, he'll usually jump straight to the conversational aspect of it; the things he does when preparing to speak. However, there's much more to it worthy of your consideration.

In these next few sections I'll cover researching the company and their competition; anticipating what's on their mind and being prepared with responses; technical skills orientation and the adaptive resume; traditional and non-traditional interview locations such as offices, public restaurants, bars, and skype; the logistics of getting to the interview; making your way to the office; observing office people and interactions happening between them; the introduction and the art of small talk; sincere compliments and comments vs the full-on suck up; discerning how the company sees the progression of the interview; verbal and non-verbal gestures of understanding; noting the organization-level of the meeting room or office; your list of questions; salary, benefit, vacation, and training discussions; next steps; the thank you note or email; evaluating the interview; and the art of pursuing multiple options and the no harm, no foul outlook. Yes, there's a here lot of good stuff to consider.

Researching The Company

Companies are like a box of chocolates. You never know what you're going to get. Each has its own set of positive and negative attributes. And there are a lot of sources for learning things you'll want to know prior to accepting employment. Researching a company prior to an interview is vitally important because it gives you a foundation for the conversation that happens when you meet.

That's right, the interview is actually a conversation; not an interrogation. Sure, they will ask questions to get a feel for the cut of your jib- their determination of the kind of personality and skills you would bring to their organization. However, they fully expect you to ask them questions too.

In researching the prospective company, the obvious first step is to conduct a web search. Viewing their website will help you learn of their divisions, locations, products and services, and you'll oftentimes even find profiles of their senior management team. Their website gives you all the information *they want you to see-* all the good things with a most positive spin.

Take full opportunity on their site to learn at a high level about their products and services and in more detail about the things this location does. Become familiar with their customers- to whom and how they sell the things they produce. And learn the names of their partners if possible to get a feel for the market.

Beyond that, a Google search will reveal other interesting information. This may include news stories of:

- Upcoming partnerships: representing potential career growth opportunity.

- Good and bad sales statistics: Hinting at expansion or even closing of the very location you'll visit.

- Recent and pending law suits: Displaying the company's vulnerability and agility in defending itself.

- Senior management transitions: They may have recently hired some superstars. However too many management changes over a short period of time, say, four chief information officers (CIOs) in five years, could indicate shifts in business direction or perhaps that they are intellectually adrift and have no clue what they are doing.

Considering whether or not to join a company is a bit like going to an amusement park for the first time, seeing a wooden roller coaster and trying to decide if it's going to be an awesome experience or something that's going to make you toss your lunch. Research, take notes, and be ready to talk about the things you find; good and bad.

Transmuting Anxiety Into Happy Anticipation

Anxiety or "experiencing failure in advance," as author Seth Godin defines it, is a perfectly normal thing; especially for people just starting in their careers. Learning to dance with your feelings is a skill, one you can master by just pushing forward. Think about it. How did LeBron James get good at basketball? He did it by playing basketball. How did you improve your engineering knowledge? You did it by studying engineering. And so it is with interviewing.

Early on in my career, an engineer friend and I decided to get together to interview each other. We each found a position we wanted, gave a print out of it and our resume to the other person, and conducted mock interviews. Let me tell you, it was one of the best things we could have done. We became more practiced in answering the kinds of technical and non-technical questions we thought we'd hear in our interviews. And this kind of exercise is even better if you can include a third, non-technical person for it's those kinds of people who come up with the fun yet truly weird questions you really can't anticipate. This practice is a rehearsal and I promise you it will go *no* more smoothly than LeBron trying to make a layup shot when he was in the fourth grade- at least the first time or two. And then, guess what? You'll get better and better and reach the point where you can't wait to meet these interviewers and potential real-world friends.

When you first walk into the company's office and meet the receptionist, appreciate that an hour ago she was at home making breakfast. And the manager you're about to meet- an hour ago he was bent over trying to tie his shoe. They are just.. like.. you.

As you would like them to be interested in you joining their team, they would like to make a happy acquaintance who becomes a great team member. *In social media terms, I treat an interview like an in-person friend request. And when you are the one reaching out in friendship, you can feel great as a person for having made them the offer to friend you back.* This is how I create happy anticipation- it's just that easy.

Anticipating What's On Their Mind

During the interview process, companies are mostly trying to determine these things:

- Do you have a solid technical grasp of the tools and methods needed to do the job?

  The tools the company utilizes are usually in the job description. Are they a Java shop? Do they use Visual Studio? How about databases? Is it MySql, SQL Server, or something else? Did they list any tools new to you? Could you do a little research on those and describe how they are connected to the other tools in creating solutions?

  Perhaps you can. Perhaps you cannot. *Be truthful no matter what.* If you try to fake your way through it, their technical team will bust you and reject your application out of hand for being untrustworthy.

- Are you intellectually curious about new technology?

  Over time, technology evolves. Read a little about updates coming to the tools they use. Be prepared to discuss at a high level how these tools have improved over time and what you like about those enhancements. The managers and technical people with whom you'll interview will have seen these too and your mentioning them creates a shared bond of the experience. They will smile back at you a little and think, "Ah, he knows." And this is a good thing.

- Are you a good listener and follower? Do you have an agreeable personality suited to taking direction?

  Be prepared to talk about your team experiences and how you like the team approach to solving challenges. The vast majority of the time you'll be working on collaborative efforts that can only be successful when people work together.

  You may also be asked to talk about one of your projects that didn't go as planned; one that failed. This is a fun, yet tricky question. The person asking it isn't at all interested in whose fault it was. The interviewer wants to hear if you are describing the experience as one where your team learned from it and got better. If someone else was to blame, he wants to hear how you describe that. Saying, "Engineer Bob was lazy and produced crap" is the worst kind of response. It's made by the kind of person who has not learned how to be tactful, one who plays the blame game, and will toss people under the proverbial bus in a heartbeat. "We were resource challenged" is a much better response. Sure, the listener will laugh, you'll laugh, and he'll get the hint.

  And if a problem was your fault, own it. For example: "In building our class I didn't realize the level of abstraction that was needed so it didn't work exactly as we expected. However, I worked with our tech lead and together we came up with a better model." Now this kind of response is perfect. It shows you owning a problem and working as part of a team to overcome it. See the value in describing it this way? *In the real world, that's what teams do.*

- Do you clean up well? Meaning, did you dress and groom properly for the interview.

  Wear a nice, clean, business-oriented suit. They may well be a dress-down, jeans type of shop, however, you get one chance to make a first impression. Unless the interview is at an unusual off-site location you should dress to impress. It doesn't need to be an expensive outfit, just a well-maintained one.

- Do you have fresh breath?

Other than body odor, yes I understand this goes without mentioning to most people, but other than body odor, bad breath is the quickest way to make someone end a conversation. Chewing gum can help but that "chomp, chomp, chomp" of it is a major distraction. So, don't chew gum. Breath mints work every time. Just pop a couple of them in your mouth after you've checked in and are waiting to meet.

- Do you have a copy of your resume?

The company with whom you'll interview has reviewed it. However, they may not have shared it with some of the team members you'll meet. Therefore, it's a great idea to bring an extra four or five clean copies in a folder.

- Did you bring a small notepad and a pen or do you have a phone app available to take notes?

During the interview the company will provide some great information, answer a bunch of your good questions, and may even ask you for additional information. For these reasons, I like to bring a very small notepad to jot down information. These can be found at most dollar stores and are only a few inches by a few inches and fit into most any pocket.

- Did you turn your phone volume to zero so it won't interrupt the conversation?

Do that.

Technical Skills Orientation

The likelihood of finding a position perfectly-matched to your existing resume can be a challenge and this is just a fact of life. One of the tactics I've regularly and successfully employed is to adapt my resume to the position for which I'm applying. In fact, there have been times when job hunting I've had as many as four distinct versions of my resume out there.

For example, if a potential position requires someone with a lot of database development I have reorganized the verbiage or words describing my work experience to go into a little more depth on my database projects. *As long as the information is truthful and you are able to effectively converse about the experience, this tactic is perfectly acceptable.* As you complete projects, look for opportunities to learn new techniques and related development tasks. For example, if you're writing the front end to a web site, ask about helping with business and database class development and vice versa. If you're writing database classes, ask about helping to author the stored procedures and functions they call too. If you are working for a small to medium sized company you may have no choice but to branch out- so be thankful. If you are working for a larger company, this kind of related work might be parceled out to a related team and you might need to volunteer to help. Once you've built a good reputation doing the development you normally do, your willingness to help another team is more easily accepted and eventually embraced. Soon enough you'll have those extra skills and can employ this tactic effectively.

There is great tradition in the United States Marine Corps, for example, of doing exactly this. When the chips are down, the Marines don't sit back and wait for good things to happen. Rather they improvise, adapt, and overcome to achieve objectives and earn success. *You can too!*

Interview Locations

In the earlier part of your career the majority of interviews you'll experience will be in traditional office locations. You'll meet a receptionist, wait in the lounge area, and eventually someone will take you to an office or a meeting room. During an interview, you may be shuttled from office to office to meet multiple people or if the interview is in in a meeting room, other people may come and go. As you gain work experience and apply for more senior positions the locations in which you recruited and where you are interviewed can change dramatically.

For example, when I gained about six years of experience, I applied for a consulting position. The gentleman recruiting me had good technical experience himself and interviewed me over the phone. I was in Reston, Virginia and he was in San Diego, California at the beach. In a folding chair with his feet in the water, we both laughed as I mentioned hearing the surf in the background. And then he started hammering me with technical questions about the use of Microsoft's Visual Studio- how to create proxies for references to Web APIs, about the differences between SQL stored procedures and triggers, primary keys vs. foreign keys, inner joins, outer joins, and why Cartesian products are bad. *Good times.* The preparation I'd done combined with the rapport we'd built about the beach helped earn me the job.

Another time, also while I was living in Reston, I found myself at a local sports bar frequented by technology folks during happy hour. *The recruiter was very slick.* A few of us were hanging out, people watching and having a good time, and the topic naturally shifted to what we were doing. My turn came and I let slip that I had successfully completed testing my C++ recursive binary tree algorithm that statistically evaluated the likelihoods particular entities were in a given geographical area based on a myriad data inputs.

Suddenly, a wiry man in a smart-looking Yves Saint-Laurent suit, his tie loosened for happy hour, moved towards us with the ease of a seasoned sports car salesman coming in for the kill. We let his obviousness slide as we were seasoned geeks with incredible confidence, this was our turf, and the frequency of this kind of thing happening had become almost comical. It was the late 1990's and the middle of the .COM boom. He gave us his practiced grin, shared a little techno-recruiting story about how good talent was hard to find, and that he had a bevy of clients looking for engineers just like us. *Sure, why not.* A couple of us interviewed right there- jovial in spirit and adult beverages in hand. *Sometimes it happens that easily- but not always.*

About Skype interviews- they happened then and do to this day. Having seen a number of funny memes about people taking selfies with their messy apartment in the background, I luckily recognized the importance of cleaning up beforehand. And I was happy I did. I dressed as if it were an in-person meeting and Skyped with a clean office in the background. The conversation went well and towards the end the interviewer complimented me on being so organized. Little things can make all the difference!

Along your career path you are going to make friends you'll want to keep long term. You'll connect on a project or even LinkedIn through common interests for example and down the line they'll hit you up. This too happened to me. One of my friends had moved on to work for a direct competitor of ours, and now that competitor wanted me too. As the industry we were in was regionally-concentrated and a lot of people knew others in it, they wanted to keep our meeting on the down low. So we met at a local restaurant. Over a casual lunch with my friend and one of the vice presidents, we discussed the state of the business and how I helped lead a team approach to solving our challenges. That was all he needed to hear. Boom. Done. Hired on the spot. *Sometimes it happens that easily- but not always.*

Tip: The idea here is to adapt to the environment of the interview. Dress and act appropriately to the locale. And don't sweat it. It's just a conversation.

Getting To The Interview

Getting to the place of an interview sounds simple enough. You take the address, enter it into Google Maps or your car's navigation system, and off you go right? Perhaps, perhaps not. Before an interview I like to make a dry run finding and getting to the location; especially if I've never been there before. There are a lot of things that can throw off the time it will take. These include traffic, construction, whether or not the parking lot is full. And if taking a train or bus, the schedule and possible maintenance comes into play.

If you are utilizing public transportation, consider taking the run scheduled ahead of the one you think you'd want to take. This offers the advantage of offsetting any scheduling or mechanical difficulties and if you are early you can do a little note review and some people watching. People watching outside of a prospective company can be quite insightful. You can see how many people show up early and how many come running in late, note the cleanliness and develop a perception of the safety of the area. If taking public transportation, note the cleanliness of the vehicle and of the people on it.

If there is a particularly funky-smelling person onboard, immediately move away from him. The last thing you want is to transport industrial-strength funk into your interview. Little things like that are noticeable.

And if you arrive super early, you can also notice whether or not there are breakfast options nearby like bagel shops or food trucks- something seen more in large cities than in rural areas. Not that you're going to take advantage of them, just make a mental note for future reference.

About breakfast: the morning of the interview play it safe. Go easy on the garlic and onions and brush your teeth before you leave the house. Should this need to be written in a book like this? Well, for some folks going on their first interview every bit of advice helps.

The other reason for not eating on the way there is that it eliminates the risk of getting something like cheese sauce on your shirt. Obviously you want to look your best so mitigate the risk of a mess; just remove it from the equation.

Observing Office People

Ahead of going in to the interview, plant a little seed in your mind to watch things going on in the office. Observe how people interact and consider- are they being friendly to each other? Do they seem generally happy and organized or does the place seem to be in a state of chaos? What you see, is what you'll get.

That is, the level of professionalism or lack of it you see at that time should be considered part and parcel of who they are as a company. Don't expect it to change much from what you see. If what you see looks bad and they tell you a story that it's not normally like that, na, na, na, na- *don't buy it. Bad behaviors are triggered, they don't just happen.*

I write from my personal experience of having heard such it's-not-normally-like-that-here stories only to later find myself swimming in a mucky, unprofessional, emotional swamp of immature man-children wishing I'd listened to my inner voice. So please listen to yours.

Your work will be challenging and the need to be dedicated to it so important that you won't have time to get caught up in petty things. Conversely, should you see the company's employees getting along great, smiling, and collaborating to get things done then definitely take note of that as well. That's the kind of place you would be lucky to find.

The Introduction And The Art Of Small Talk

When you arrive for the interview, it's customary to check in with the company receptionist. Companies usually have each visitor sign into a log book; name, time of arrival, and the person one has come to visit. For interviewees, it's also common have them fill out job application paperwork. So it's a good idea to show up a good ten minutes ahead of time just in case.

Befriend the receptionist- give her a big smile and say hello. Let her know the person you've come to see and comment on how nice a day it is. Mention something nice about their building or the like. Show some happiness. *People like happy people.*

When the person with whom you've come to interview comes to you, stand up, smile, look him in the eyes, and extend your hand to shake his. Grasp his hand firmly but not any stronger than he is giving you. And don't let that handshake turn into an Incredible Hulk testosterone challenge of who can grip more strongly. You want the person to see you as engaging, confident, and happy to make his acquaintance.

From there you will be lead to the place where you will speak together. It might be a conference room right near the receptionist's office or back to a place where people in their department sit.

When you enter the room, look to see if the other person has a seat in mind for himself. Let him have first choice at a seat and go from there. And when you do take a seat, sit up with good posture and do not slouch. Keep your head up and engage in good eye contact. Don't look down or away much. People who maintain good eye contact are perceived to be interested in the conversation. People who stare up at the ceiling or away are perceived to be mentally someplace else. *Stay in the moment.*

The interviewer will likely thank you for coming in and ask you how it's going. Be positive. And not just during the introduction. A positive attitude can go a long way to winning someone over. A positive response might be, "Yes, it's great to meet you too and thank you for investing the time to chat."

Notice I used the word "chat" and not "interview." The word "interview" can have an adversarial connotation or feeling. Where the word "chat" is much more friendly- like it's an exchange of information and ideas. And that's all this meeting is. Also notice the use of the word "investing"- the interviewer's time is being consumed. *Investing his time hints to him that it will be well worth it.*

Now look around the room. If it's the interviewer's office there will likely be things in it he values as important. Do you see a college diploma or sign? Do you see a sports team logo? How about a family picture, where they are involved in some activity? Is there a window with a nice view? There will likely be something in the office about which you can make a short, positive comment. Look for these things. Little supportive comments will usually garner a smile because you've shown interest and at least taken his mind, even if momentarily, off his busy day. You still have to step up in the question and answer portion of the meeting but small bonding moments add value too. They show you as personable and likeable.

Sincere Comments

People can recognize shallow compliments a mile away. The small bonding discussed in the previous section is a sincere one, meaning the comment is intended to demonstrate appreciation of a thing while not putting the recipient on a pedestal. Here are two examples:

Example One:

"Ah, you attended Virginia Tech. They have a strong engineering reputation." – This is a sincere comment about the quality of the program. Did the person do well there? You don't know and you don't care. It's a comment about Virginia Tech itself.

Example Two:

"Oh cool, you attended Virginia Tech. They only admit the best and the brightest." – This is a total suck-up comment. It's shallow, obvious nature would make any intelligent recipient feel uneasy. This uneasiness would translate into not trusting the person making the comment. Notice the difference?

Further, people who have somehow found their way onto an engineering team who make these kinds of suck-up comments are not at all trusted by their fellow team members. Persistently adding engineering value and supporting your team's efforts to do the same will skyrocket the likelihood of you fitting in as an appreciated member of the team.

Tip: Yes-men, boot-lickers, butt-kissers, brown-nosers, panderers, minions, puppets, toadies, and other sycophants suck up to the boss and add no true value to the business proposition. They are easily noticed by their fellow team members and actively shunned. Don't be one. Carefully consider the kinds of supportive comments you offer and you will earn peer respect.

Interview Progression

Once the little bit of small talk has transpired, the rest of the conversation begins. And it usually goes like this:

- You will be asked about your current company and why you are looking for a new position.

  This tells them if you got fired, are just curiously looking, and indicates your level of desperation to find work. It also hints to them how flexible they might need to be in salary and benefits negotiation.

  If this is your first job after college, don't sweat the salary and benefits too much. The experience you'll gain far outweighs the extra thousand or two you might be able to squeeze out of them.

However, if you are a more seasoned engineer, you should do your best to play this off as your being curious and interested in the opportunity but not desperate.

- You will be asked how you applied the tools listed in the job description.

Most development tools can be applied to meet many different kinds of business needs. The goal of this question is to provide a starting point around which more specific technical questions can be answered. If one of your more involved projects was building a Web API that fed into a relational database where you also built an SSIS package that ETL'd into a data warehouse then he knows which technical questions to ask you. Get it?

- You will be asked some applied-technical questions- a deeper dive into your application of these in the business of business.

Extending the example in the previous paragraph, the interviewer could ask, "Can you tell me more about that project?"

At this point you would describe your participation in the design and authoring of the Web API interface specification document and the people with whom you negotiated- business partners who called the Web API's methods, other developers within your company, a database developer team on the ETL portion, and the QA team for example. You might further describe how you supported integrated testing in working with the QA team and the external partners using the Web API you developed. In these answers you'd describe test harnesses you built, datasets you helped create through custom queries, and more.

Your goal in answering these next-level-deeper questions is to describe the ways you used these tools to connect teams in furthering the project's goals.

- You will be asked even more questions to determine the breadth and depth of your technical knowledge.

Now that the interviewer appreciates your understanding of strongly-typing and loosely-coupling interacting components, he wants to determine the strength of your technical grasp. Extending the example again, he would ask, "Now can tell me how you connected the Web API to the database?"

Here you might explain in decent detail that you created a business class with methods called by the Web API endpoint. And you further abstracted the solution to include a database class- a class with properties and methods that served as a black box service provider of database functionality. From there you created methods that instantiated database objects, established a connection to the database, further set connection and command properties to facilitate the execution of parameterized stored procedures, ensured your connections were eventually closed, and how the class handled errors- whether each method was wrapped in a try-catch-finally block or you created a custom base class that handled errors you let bubble up.

These are the points where the rubber meets the road so to speak- where they know if you know what you're claiming you know. If you know things, describe the things you know. And if you don't, then don't try to fake you're way through it.

The vast majority of the time, a company will send their best technical folks to meet with candidates- and their bovine excrement detectors are usually well tuned. Do your best, be honest, and don't sweat it.

Only pseudo-intellectual techno-zealots discount someone, for example, if his internship in object oriented development was in Java vs Visual C#. If the interviewer gets really cranky about that and you are applying for a position for which you're otherwise qualified, then you should question the idea of working for them. They'll likely be unnecessarily picky about a lot of things.

In my experience, the more seasoned the technical interviewer, the more he'll also appreciate theoretical concepts. You see, anyone can learn how to use an integrated development environment (IDE) and even those can be used in multiple ways to achieve the same objectives. However, it's more important to understand the theory, for example, of object oriented design and development than have memorized every sub-menu's context-sensitive modal dialog options. One could understand a lot of the functionality of Visual Studio and still produce an un-scalable, inefficient work product. These deeper-level technical questions are where you demonstrate that you also understand bigger picture and theory.

- The person will ask about some difficult challenges you've encountered and how you overcame them.

The *what-was-hard-for-you* kind of question has caught more than one interviewee off guard. These are interesting ones and there are a couple of levels on which the response is judged. On the first level, there are two kinds of problems- individual things you didn't know and perhaps had to research and group project things that got tangled up. An example of an individual challenge might be, say, that you'd never written a web interface that allowed users to upload files and so you had to research that. In this case, hypothetically, one might describe how he leveraged the StackOverflow and MSDN websites to see best-practice ways to do it.

This kind of answer shows you are proactive, that you won't sit there like a lost puppy and instead have that self-starter nature to just go figure things out. It also shows that you respect the larger developer community and recognize others face similar challenges and one can learn from their experiences too.

An example of a group project challenge might be that you had an intractable partner company with a stronger political and financial position in your project who refused to adhere to your company's interface specifications so you raised this issue to your manager who successfully negotiated for more time to develop a special interface just for them.

This kind of answer shows your ability to recognize non-technical roadblocks and diplomatically raise them to your boss for supportive resolution. It shows you as a team player capable of seeing the role diplomacy plays in successful projects.

On a second level here, there is the notion beyond your having an individual or group project issue- that you experienced an issue and are open enough to share your thoughts on it. Some engineers, especially less experienced ones, are shy about giving an answer at all to a question like this for fear it might show weakness.

Let me tell you here and now, it just isn't true. Demonstrating your ability to overcome obstacles is considered a strength.

How do you think engineering directors and vice presidents got to be directors and vice presidents? It was by leading and helping their teams solve interesting challenges. Irrespective of whether you are the newest newbie-McNoob or the team's technical lead- when you are on a team, you have the opportunity to add value.

If you are a seasoned developer applying for a position, then the interviewer would expect you to have an answer to this kind of question. However, if you are freshly out of college, fret not. The interviewer knows full well you don't have years of experience under your belt. And you are likely interviewing for an entry level position so in this case, feel free to talk about a challenge you experienced in a summer internship or even a college group project. It's all good.

- The person will ask what aspects of your job you've really enjoyed.

Answering the question about the aspects of engineering work you enjoy affords you the chance to reveal a little of your personality. Engineers are often introverts- people who enjoy the solitude of digging into research and development on their own. While this can be fun, one can find himself exuberantly jumping for joy on finding a malloc-related memory leak to a completely empty room. Perhaps at this point you can see where I'm going.

Joy is best experienced with others. And the way you discuss what you like about your experiences reveals your level of interest in interacting with others; the others who already work there.

In my experience, the larger the company, the more easy it is for one with a STEM degree to opt for a business-oriented career track versus an engineering one. For example, when I interned at Bell Communications Research in New Jersey these two tracks were clearly defined. I was added to an office that had two gentlemen; both with STEM degrees. The one who was on the business track spent much of his day in planning meetings with people inside and outside of the company. There they collected business requirements and translated them into carefully and precisely worded technical ones, but they didn't actually build things. The other office mate had his PhD and was on the technical track. As I mentioned earlier in the book, he came to work wearing jeans, flip-flops, and a Batman tee shirt. He was extremely intelligent, had a hilarious personality, and did theoretical and applied parallel processing algorithm development. And each loved his role. Together they were an odd couple- each master of his domain and yet they'd become fast friends who liked to joke and bounce ideas off each other. In our big, beautiful science-oriented world, there's plenty of room for different kinds of technology people and in this circle I consider them all engineers.

It takes a certain level of career maturity to be comfortable in whom you are and where you want to be. Once you find it, the joy of what you do starts to shine through and you become incredibly charismatic.

When a company asks you the what-did-you-like question, they're trying to understand your personality. Are you an introvert? An extrovert? That helps them determine if you'd be a good fit for the position or group for which you are interviewing or perhaps another one.

They just want to get to know you. So smile, and just be you.

Verbal And Non-verbal Gestures

While you are enjoying the conversation, some subtle and not so subtle indicators of how things are going will make themselves known. These can aid you in determining whether to keep going with your train of thought or to adjust the content of what you are saying. While you are answering each question, look to see if the other person is smiling or frowning, expressing interest or confusion, nodding his head up and down or shaking it left and right. Each of these indicates whether or not the person values the response being given- whether or not you are on the right track with what you are saying.

If he is really interested or agreeing with what you are saying, he may lean forward, consistently make eye contact, and smile. If he disagrees with what you are saying or you're talking too much he may look up to the ceiling, check his watch, shake his head, or attempt to cut you off. Notice these things and adjust your responses as needed. Entire books have been written around body language and *reading the room* and invite you to check them out further if the topic is of interest to you. I mention it here to help you become aware that reading body language is an effective tactic in helping you guide the flow of the meeting. This is meant to be a friendly conversation; available to be enjoyed both ways.

Don't be shy about showing your happiness. Smile, a lot. And look for opportunities to spin conversational points in positive ways. I'll write it again- people like happy, positive people on their team so let the sterling aspects of your personality shine through. Commit yourself to maintaining a positive outlook in the interview- and always while at work. It will get you, and every team you're on, through the hard times.

Noting The Organization

Now this isn't all about them. You are evaluating the company itself and this person as a prospective boss or coworker. What you see in the interviewer's office should be considered their "normal." *They are showing you who they are.*

Is the office super clean and organized? This is a good sign that they are professional and care about how they are perceived. If it's a meeting room, what you see is exactly what one would expect their clients to see. Over the years I've been an engineering manager and hired and fired dozens and dozens of professionals. And I've always invested the time to ensure our interview place was clean and free from distractive things. It's how professional companies operate.

Are you in the engineering manager's office? How organized is it? How clean is it?

Having neat stacks of papers is one thing. Having a shamblized mess quite another. You'll be able to tell the difference.

Does the office have a coffee cup or soda can visible? Not an issue, that happens all the time. Are there abandoned food or candy wrappers and crumbs lying about? Well, that's not good. You'll need to decide for yourself if any bad things you see are outweighed by the opportunity itself. Or, conversely, if all the good you're seeing is flat-out impressive.

Your List Of Questions

If the conversation is going well, the interviewer will afford you the opportunity to ask him some questions. This is usually a sign you are still being considered for the position- not that you have it locked up but that you're in the running. And if you are still interested in it, you've now got the responsibility to not mess it up. Asking the wrong or right questions can help tip the balance one way or the other. So let's consider some wrong and right questions.

Here are a few wrong questions that could take you out of the running:

- Looks like you're using a Microsoft OS. Can I get a Mac?

- What's it take to get an office instead of a cubicle?

- How soon can I get a raise?

- How often does the company conduct drug tests? And are they announced ahead of time?

- Does the company do background checks?

- Does the company monitor our email?

- I've got a lot going on, what's the company's work from home policy?

- How might I eventually get promoted out of this position or department?

- What's the policy about working for a competitor?

So what's *wrong* with these questions? When you work for a company you are serving at their convenience and you'll be permitted to stay as long as it's convenient for them. *Each of these questions though is selfish- not selfless. Not one of them supports the company's mission. Make no mistake- they are on a mission to serve clients.* And unless they're a non-profit they also exist to earn that profit. The questions above show the person asking them to be a difficult with whom to deal, representing a risky proposition for the organization.

Put simply, an interviewer hearing these kinds of questions will think the person asking them could be untrustworthy and a pain in the butt. And just as software projects run best when all the thrashing and analysis happens in the beginning, it's also true that the interview is the company's best chance of avoiding downstream employee problems.

Now let's consider some of the right questions for you to ask:

- What are some of the things you really like about working for the company?

- Does the department do some team building things like lunch and learn or have a sports team?

- What do you think are some of the challenges facing the department and company?

- Can you talk a little about the culture of the company? Do we freely interact with other departments for example? Are most people on a first name basis?

- Can you talk about the company's plan and direction for the next few years? Are we, *and yes I use the word "we" on purpose,* expanding markets or product lines?

- Most companies evaluate new employees for an amount of time once they start. Can you talk a little about your early expectations should I earn this opportunity?

So what's *right* about these questions? *Each one is unabashedly selfless; putting the various teams and company first. And each question expresses the desire of the person asking it to connect on a personal level for the good of the company.* These questions show the person asking them as interested in the longer-term, greater good, and a person who wants to be a part of a team that helps make things even better.

Some might call these questions softballs or easy to answer. Well, they are if the interviewer hits them out of the figurative ballpark. However, there are plenty of companies in which the chaotic physical and personnel mess you may have witnessed to this point will be negatively reinforced by the interviewer's inability to answer them well. Meaning, if the company seems like a bit of a mess and the interviewer has no good or positive answers to easy questions like these then your perception of them being an *actual mess* is likely true. So take it as a further red flag.

If you are okay with what you've seen and learned about the company, and the interviewer puts a positive spin on these kinds of questions- then it might actually be as nice a place as it seems. Let your intuition and gut feeling guide you based on what you see and hear.

Salary Discussions

Negotiating salary for one's first position after college is very different than doing so for the second job and beyond. This is because your innate value or what you are bringing to the table is meaningfully different as your experience grows.

If you are about to seek your first position out of college I reaffirm that you consider two things. First, the value of the knowledge and experience you will gain early in your career is more important than the salary itself. In your first position you're going to adapt to working in the real world, begin solving real-world problems, and will come to understand better ways to help people. The engineering theory you learned in college will be tempered or enhanced, over time, with actual business experience. And the skills you'll build will serve as a foundation in your becoming a solid techno-diplomat. Secondly, we're talking about an entry level position; one designed for people with a degree yet little or no experience. This means the rule of supply and demand comes into play- meaning if you are too difficult with your first company on salary it will be relatively easy for them to ignore you and choose someone else who also has little to no experience.

Therefore, I'd focus more on making the right company size selection- as mentioned in the large versus small discussion earlier in this book. If you feel sure this company is where you want to start, and their offer is reasonable, just smile and accept it. Then soak up all that good experience to build up your people skills. Once you've established yourself, which might take two to three years, you can reevaluate the company, its opportunities, opportunities outside this company, and decide if you are ready to leapfrog to a more challenging position.

Company salary over the first three years, to me, feels a lot like a compressed home loan. In the beginning they are paying you too much for your actual worth- you know little to nothing about their industry or the real business world. But by the end of the third year you will have learned a lot and their raises usually haven't kept up with your true worth at that point. Therefore, it's common for really skilled people to notice this and jump to a new company if intellectual challenges and interesting opportunities are lacking.

If this is your second company or beyond and you are bringing to the table some solid software development and helpful business experience, the law of supply and demand begins to tilt more in your favor. This is especially true if you've got some good recommendations and have built up a network on a website like *LinkedIn.com*. In this case I recommend you leverage that skillset and experience and negotiate for a salary as close to the positon maximum as possible. Learning their upper salary bound can be a challenge. If it was listed in the job posting then you're going to be able to judge your skills and experience against the position. The stronger you match it or even exceed it in some areas, the higher you can negotiate towards the maximum. And don't be afraid of getting close to that salary upper bound if you're a strong candidate because in the technology world that maximum moves upward most every year due to inflation and the fact there is a shortage of good engineers.

Now if the company doesn't list the salary maximum you can do something similar but different. *Others might invite you to look at the national averages for these positions but I strongly advise against that.* The reason is that the salary for a mid-level engineer in New York, Philadelphia, Atlanta, Dallas, Silicon Valley, or any large city is much higher than the same positon in a little, dinky town out in the middle of nowhere. So what's the definition of *out in the middle of nowhere?* Look at a big map. Now choose any city and take a string measuring to scale fifty miles. Using the city as the center point, draw a circle from the other end point of the string. Outside that circle may be beautiful country- but it's also far enough away that it fits the definition of small; where salaries are less than the average and aren't competitive. If the company is in the middle of nowhere, the average salary can give you an unrealistically high expectation and asking for it you can price you out of the position. If the company is near or in a big city, a request for that average salary could have you leaving money on the table because in the big city demand outstrips supply and companies will generally pay higher than the average. Get it? The good news is there is a way to navigate this.

Open a web browser to your favorite engineering jobs website. Now search for similar positions within twenty miles that do happen to list a salary. If you are looking at public sector government or non-profit positions then take a small average of those. If you are looking at private companies then take a small average of those. Segmenting them this way is intentional because, generally speaking, private companies pay higher salaries.

Let me give you a specific example. Back in 2003, Children's Hospital Of Philadelphia (CHOP) gave me a verbal offer to become a permanent employee at the salary of $85,000. Located in Philadelphia, CHOP employees were subject to a 3.92% city wage tax; not CHOP's fault, just a fact of life. MediMedia USA of Yardley, Pennsylvania offered me $100,000 to start, there was no city wage tax, and benefits seemed about the same. CHOP was non-profit, MediMedia was a for-profit company. I've experienced this kind of wage gap many times over and this is just one example of the difference. So it's important when determining the salary you desire to compare apples to apples if you will.

Suggesting seasoned engineers negotiate for the best salary they can get is my attempt to limit exposure to *Zeno's paradox* of never achieving the maximum salary possible; something I'll explain in just a little bit.

Once you are in the position, the company has you right where they want you and perhaps need you. The companies for whom I've worked based raises each year on the following factors:

- How well the company performed- something you really don't know and certainly cannot control.

- How well your department performed- something you might know and can influence but not totally control.

- How much money the company put into the budget for raises- something you don't know and cannot control.

- How well you performed- something completely within your ability to control.

- How easy you are to replace- something based on what you bring to the table compared to the law of supply and demand.

- The likelihood of them losing you- something they think they know based on your skillset, outlook, and gregarious nature. Average, introverted employees serve their purpose and won't go anywhere, where outgoing superstars are a rare find and in high demand everywhere.

Now back to our Greek philosopher friend, Zeno. In my experience, if you're doing a solid job in your current position, the company implements what I call **Zeno's Salary Dichotomy Paradox.** That is, in your first year you'll receive a decent raise; say four percent. In your second year, that drops to two percent. And in the third year, that drops to one percent. As the raise amount divides in half each year you never actually reach the maximum for the position.

Now there could be a couple of reasons for this. On the one hand, once you reach it there's no monetary challenge left; you're maxed out. On the other more-likely hand it's reasonable to expect an employee to have the drive to seek a larger, more responsible role in the organization over time. And not showing as much love in the form of an annual raise for someone doing the exact same job he did last year represents a financial kick in in the butt to get employees to seek that additional responsibility.

Tip: Zeno's Salary Dichotomy Paradox is an axiom I feel applies to entry level hires as well as seasoned ones. In each case the employee can meaningfully increase his salary by taking on additional responsibility while honing his interpersonal skills. Hopefully these concepts prove insightful and useful for you.

Benefit Discussions

Every private and public company for which I've worked operated the same way. Each had a single medical insurance provider who offered multiple levels or plans priced based on coverage. The more they covered, the more it cost. The same was true with dental insurance. However, with dental there were usually only two levels- "cheapo dental" and "the good plan." And even the good plan didn't cover everything; braces being an example.

As a side note, the fallacy of insurance is in full view when it comes into dental. You see, insurance companies are in business to make a profit. The only way they can do that is if they skim money off the top of your premium and not pay it to the service provider. They try to gamble you won't actually use it and you gamble that you will. It's easy to see in dental plan descriptions how they limit what they cover so, in the end, the insurance company wins. Now most dentists with whom I've dealt were fine negotiating much lower fees for patients who pay cash, however, most patients don't have the patience to engage in that- especially when they are in pain and need a root canal. At that point the dentist office has the advantage, because they know you are in pain. Nobody goes in six months ahead of time, individually, and tries to negotiate a rate for something they might need down the line. My advice? Buy and utilize the best dental plan they offer. And as for medical- that really depends on your individual situation.

Both medical and dental company plans are organized well before you arrive and you'll just select within those offerings.

Holidays And Vacation

Every company celebrates a set of national holidays and this can vary a little from company to company. The interesting trend I've noticed with America becoming an even more diverse melting pot of culture is the adoption of more floating holidays. *A floating holiday is one you can take anytime you like.* It still needs to be scheduled with your supervisor but you can take it to celebrate a time meaningful to you and your family. This flexibility has made floating holidays very popular among employees.

Now let's think about vacation. Almost all companies have a fixed two week vacation policy when it comes to new employees with little to no experience. However, the amount of vacation available generally grows with the level of employee experience. For example, after say four to five years of experience it's common to earn a third week of vacation. And after ten to fifteen years a fourth week is often provided.

Vacation though is treated a little differently than salary. Salary is a precise number, easily identifiable in the company's bottom line equation. Vacation relates to productivity. And department-level productivity can be an ungainly beast to quantify; meaning hard to measure. If your experience represents a solid investment for the company, meaning they'd like to hire you, and your previous company gave you X weeks off or your level of experience is reasonably close to the threshold where you'd receive it then definitely ask for that level of vacation. Never go backwards with respect to vacation and if you are close, ask for the next level up. This is also a good test of how much they value you. If the hiring manager really likes you, he'll fight for you to have the time off.

Fact: Salary might be an area tough for them to negotiate but vacation is oftentimes more easy to justify and easier to hide in the company's bottom line.

It's also common for companies to offer "sick time." This is time off when the employee is actually sick. Mostly due to the fact it's difficult to define "sick" and not every time one is sick does he go to the doctor and get a note, companies have been shifting to using what is called "PTO" or personal time off. PTO is a combination of vacation time and sick time. The vacation time can sometimes be negotiated, the sick time cannot. For example, this year I earned three weeks of vacation PTO and one week sick PTO for a total of four weeks. At our company, these can be taken in segments of four hours or whole days. So, if you happened to have eaten some bad sushi at lunch you could take four hours of the afternoon as PTO. Likewise, you might need to pick up relatives at the airport, far away, one day. In that case you might use or burn four hours of PTO time to do that. Your company's policy will vary slightly but for the most part employees can take PTO time in hours as long as it's recorded in their time keeping systems.

When to take vacation can also be tricky proposition. After you have been with the company for a little bit, ask about your department's policy on holiday vacation. Many companies require some staff to work over known holidays- to cover in case clients have questions. Therefore, it's a polite and common practice for American companies to ask employees to take just one of the two weeks off at the end of December, for example, so everyone can get some time off. Most departments maintain a time-off calendar online where all team members mark their requested time. This supports planning projects and other client needs. After you've been with the company a couple of months, ask your manager how the department plans time off and guidance will be provided. Then when a particular date or week is important to you, request it as early as possible to increase the likelihood of it being approved.

Training And Education

If you have earned your undergraduate STEM degree and are interested in pursuing your master's degree, chances are good you'll be able to get some kind of financial support. In my experience, certain types of companies are more likely to provide it. Those include larger government and non-profit organizations and very successful for-profit businesses. This is yet another reason for new graduates to seriously consider working for a larger organization to start.

In my opinion, expanded educational and training benefits are where government and non-profit organizations try to make up for their generally lower salary structure. They see it as a way to keep talented people. Super successful, large, for-profit companies can feel that way too, however, they are also looking to groom future leaders and scientists who will help them innovate and expand operations. Organizations and companies less-likely to offer this kind benefit are small-town governments and companies and small startup companies. They have the same needs and desires as their larger counterparts, just not the budget to support it.

The Choosing Your First Company, Large vs Small section earlier in this book discusses how some of these programs work. If the interview is going well it's fine to ask some of the following types of questions to gain a better understanding of educational benefits available to their employees:

- I'd love to contribute to helping Company X, however, I'm wondering if the engineers experience some specialized company training?

  Many companies train their employees internally quite a bit. For example, one of my previous companies required all employees to complete a week long effective communications class, another company sent me to Tennessee for to learn about programmable logic controllers, another to Ft. Lauderdale, Florida for specialized computer training, and yet another to Nashua, New Hampshire to learn how to write customized apps that integrated with a document management system. Sometimes this kind of training is a requirement and sometimes you can volunteer for it.

- Does Company X support employees attending graduate school for related degrees in software engineering or project management?

When the question is asked this way, the interviewer generally understands you're interested in more than a yes or no answer and usually more detailed information is provided. Some companies like Bell Communications Research for example, had a well-defined path to it taught by a limited number of top notch universities. Other companies are more flexible and let the employee choose as long as the degree is technical or supports the company mission. If the interviewer is familiar with the specific reimbursement information he'll tell you, otherwise he'll invite you to ask the Human Resources department representative about it and they'll give you the scoop.

- Is Company X partnered with any universities to provide free or discounted courses?

This is something I've seen quite a bit; especially with government and large non-profit organizations. They may negotiate a volume business rate with a university because so many employees are required to complete some particular courses or training.

- How long do I have to work at Company X in order to *earn* tuition assistance benefits?

You can ask this question, however, you almost don't need to ask it. If the company has a probationary period, as discussed earlier in this section, then it's customary for the employee to have to make it past that point for educational benefits to become available. If the company makes no mention of a probationary or evaluation period then you may choose to ask. And use the word *earn*- that lets them know you recognize it's a privilege.

- Is there a requirement to stay with Company X for a certain length of time after I complete my degree?

    This kind of rule is quite common. Company X would be making an investment in you and it's reasonable to expect them to want a return on that investment. I've worked in some places that wanted a three to five year commitment. I didn't necessarily have to stay in the same department after completion of my degree but would need to stay with the company itself. Completing your degree can, naturally, lead to new responsibilities and opportunities within the company as well.

When seeking information about educational and training benefits, my preference is to keep the questions as short as possible and presume nothing. *When I've gotten to this stage of the interview, the likelihood is good they want me. So I let them do as much of the talking as possible, giving the chance to sell me a little on why it's in my interest to work for them. It's also a way I test them- if they really like me they talk up this benefit, others, and how Company X is such a great team.* It's a minor test but it can be an effective one; especially for managers who can't hide their interest in you.

Completing The Interview

As the interview draws to a close, there is one thing you need to do and two more you can choose to do.

First: stand up, smile, reach out to shake the interviewer's hand, look into his eyes, and thank him for investing the time to meet with you. Note I used the word *invest*. Once again, this is intentional. When someone uses the time or takes the time, no upside for having done it is in his mind. However, when you say, "Thank you for investing the time to meet with me today, Mr. Jones," this definitely hints that there will be good return on that investment. And if you are close to having won the position, this little bit of mental topspin could help close the deal.

Second: If you are interested in the position and the interviewer asked you to provide some additional information, reiterate to him that you will provide it. "I'll make sure to provide the additional information we discussed." This lets him know you were paying attention to detail and will follow through.

Third: If you are interested in the position, make this clear. "The engineering position we discussed sounds like an exciting challenge and I'm interested in becoming part of the team." With this kind of statement there's no doubt in his mind as to your willingness to commit.

At this point the interviewee is usually escorted out of the building. So, off you go.

Next Steps

If the interviewer or company itself asked you to provide additional information, obtain it and review it carefully for spelling or grammar errors before sending it. If they asked you to take a drug test then do it. The goal here is put the ball entirely in their court so they can make a relatively quick decision.

The Thank You Note Or Email

In the olden days, prior to the internet, polite and professional job applicants followed up interviews with simple, carefully-crafted, one-page thank you letters or notes. Some people try to do it via email today but I find that much less personal. As an engineering manager, I have kept and filed the notes I've received if we had a better candidate but also liked the person who sent the note. I have, months later, reached back out to the candidate and hired him then. And in a couple of cases, after we'd teched-out a candidate, I forwarded his information to another department whose manager was also looking to hire.

The thinking is to leave the best impression possible and a little thing like a thank you note does just that.

Evaluating The Interview

As an engineering manager, I've conducted technical interviews with over a hundred candidates. In about ten percent of those, we also included a written or computer-driven test. However, the vast majority of the time the positon was complex on so many different levels that this would have been nearly impossible and so the interviews have been face to face. Additionally, it is very common these days for hiring agencies, companies that help find jobs for engineers, to utilize online testing to confirm competencies before putting candidates in front of their clients. So be ready to prove you know the languages or toolsets listed on your resume to a recruiter; before you're in front of their client- your potential employer.

The average amount of time I set aside for an interview has been about forty-five minutes. If you are interviewing with a single person, this is a pretty good yardstick. If you're going to interview with multiple people, it's reasonable to expect the total length of time to be longer. Although the length of time can vary a bit, there are some telltale signs to let you know how it's going.

As the interviewer, I had my topics outlined in advance. I knew I was going to invest ten minutes or so in each area. For example, on creating web front ends check to see if the interviewee understood how HTML controls were used. With every control there are properties and methods used most frequently and some used much less. It's the most common ones we care about- ones that trigger post backs or point to CSS style sheets for example. Then I'd check to see if the person knew about user-created controls; reusable front end code. And I'd ask whether or not the prospective developer had used popular UI (user interface) components such as those built by the company known as Telerik. *The candidate's understanding of object oriented development was usually more important to me than use of a specific toolset.* And next I'd ask about business and database class development and how the interviewee saw front end code interacting with those- knowing their previous employers may have organized this development separately or merged it together.

My goal here was to see if he understood the various parts and how they were connected in building a good quality solution. If the candidate was doing well, I'd smile, nod my head up and down, and jump ahead to a more technical question. If not, I'd pause for a second or two, tilt my head a little and squint my eyes. Usually that look alone was enough to motivate the candidate to further explain what he'd meant.

For the most part I'd give the person the benefit of the doubt. When needed, I'd try to ask the same question a different way. However, in some cases where there was only one correct response this just wasn't possible. Sometimes the person's experience or environment caused him to implement an unorthodox solution and I was okay with it provided he could explain the reasoning behind it.

When an interviewee missed two or three questions in a row or every solution he proposed was some kind of the fly-by-the-seat-of-your-pants thing, I had great pause. This generally indicated him to be clueless, dangerous, a bovine excrement artist, or all three of these. When this happened, I offered no feedback but jumped ahead to the next section. *And this, if you experience it, is a clue the interview isn't going well.*

A typical topic such as front end development or database development could take a good ten to fifteen minutes to discuss. And if the conversation is going well, the interviewer will delve even deeper into it. However, if he cuts the topic off short and changes the subject then there are two possibilities- you either did really well and convinced him or he's given up on the topic and it did not go well. *You will surely know.*

As the interviewer I made note of the candidate's weakness in an area and began to quiz on another area important to the position. If the person did well from then on, we'd consider him relative to the other candidates being interviewed. It was exactly like choosing teams on the kid's playground when we were little. Of the players there and available to play, we chose the best.

Now if the interviewee stumbled on a *second section*, our meeting accelerated to the endpoint. There really wasn't much use in going on and I'd save both our time, thank him for coming in, and cut it short.

So to summarize this section, if the interviewer takes a deep breath, suddenly stops asking questions in an area, starts fidgeting with his papers, and isn't smiling- you didn't do well there. If he is smiling, leaning in, or asking more questions- you my friend are on a roll.

Now if you aren't on a roll with your conversation, it's very important to remember that this isn't the end of the world. Read that again and then again.

If you didn't do well, invest some time after the interview to write down every topic and question you can remember and then go research them. It's really okay- *this* opportunity was just not the right fit at this time.

And for both good interviews and bad ones, remember to write the thank you note mentioned in the previous section. The thank you note isn't about the end-result- it's about being nice.

The No Harm, No Foul Outlook

When you see an ad for an engineering position, have you ever considered the odds the company might receive your resume and toss all the others in the trash- knowing from that one document, without having met you, that you were perfect? Here's a news flash to the 0.000001% of readers who answered, "yes": Companies bring in several candidates and evaluate them against the position and each other; never just one.

By Tom Nicholas

As an engineering manager, on more than one occasion I found two or three candidates who would have been perfectly fine for the position and we simply had to choose one. Was there any real reason, rhyme, federal or state law mandating I select one over the other? Nope.

The only thing that mattered was whether or not I thought the person was a good fit. As the hiring manager, my reputation for selecting qualified candidates was on the line and my particular selections were purely subjective. *Now that you understand companies see employees as commodities you, my talented in-demand engineer, should look at them the exact same way.* Might Company X seem like an amazing place to be? Sure. Is Company X the only game in town? Well, unless you live out in the middle of nowhere, there surely will be more than one good option worthy of your consideration. And even then, with high-speed connectivity available it's entirely possible to telecommute one hundred percent of the time. In fact, as I write this book I'm here to tell you I've been working from home for over six years. Now I do come into the office a few times a month so they will continue to recognize my face and I can meet the new people getting hired but otherwise I work from my home office.

When you are seeking a new position, consider applying to multiple companies at the same time. You may need to juggle interview times a little, telling one you have another appointment should the meeting times conflict, but there's no need to go into detail. And after the interview one company may like you a lot and try to get you to commit quickly to their offer. Now it is reasonable to ask them to give you over the weekend or two days to talk it over with your significant other or spouse. It's all part of the game. However, a company usually won't give you more than two days or over one weekend.

For skilled engineers, this isn't the 1950's where employers ruled the roost and employees just had to settle. In the age of high tech, you too have a say in the company you choose to serve. So don't be shy about applying to multiple companies at the same time. If you choose to go through a head hunter or placement agency, care must be taken to ensure two different companies don't set you up to interview with the same employer. Remember, head hunters earn from the hiring company either a flat fee or an amount equal to some percentage of your first year salary for their service of finding you. So if a second head hunter finds out from a company you've already interviewed with them via another head hunter they get kind of cranky- cranky with you. *They often ask for exclusivity for helping you.*

178

Because he is committed to providing this service, a head hunter will be happy to set you up to interview with multiple companies. All you have to do is ask him what else they have available and he'll hook you up. You are not obligated to accept the first offer that comes along if you have doubts. Since they are loyal to you, then you should be loyal to them. Turn them into friends and they'll take good care of you over time. During the years I was a consultant I had the privilege of working with several consulting head hunters who found contracts for me. And with each one I worked a few back-to-back contracts and built nice business relationships.

So what is this no harm, no foul outlook? The no harm, no foul outlook about job prospecting is the same one many authors of dating advice books provide on that topic. When you go on a first date with a person, the honest goal should be just to get to know the person- to find out what defines her, how she thinks, what makes her tic, what drives her, makes her happy, what is her passion, and how she organizes her life in pursuing it. It's not to jump ahead and presume a relationship already exists. The same is true with meeting company representatives.

The manifestation of the no harm, no foul outlook is to take things easily and not emotionally invest too heavily in the outcome of the meeting with the company. You are meeting one another to evaluate the possibilities. Sometimes it's a nice match, sometimes not. Either way, no big deal.

The likelihood is high that over the course of your career you will work for several companies. Between permanent employment and contracting I've worked with around twenty. Overt time their needs evolved and so did mine. And that's just a happy part of life. So why don't I worry?

I keep my skill set strong, my contacts on LinkedIn fresh, and live in the moment by giving my best each day. And come what may, it's no harm, no foul.

Being The New Person

The first day at a company is usually a really happy one for the new employee. Remember that feeling you experienced the first day of school each year? Everything seemed bright, clean, new, and the place had an unusually fresh scent to it. The first few days at a new company always felt like that for me. Perhaps it was my unfamiliarity with the building, meeting all these new people, or perhaps it was the lemony-fresh disinfectant that gave my desk that new-look sheen. The combination of these things and the thought I was embarking upon a new adventure with a perfectly clean slate made me as excited as a six year old opening a new Lego Kit on Christmas morning. And it will feel this way for you too.

When starting at your new company, one of the things your fellow coworkers will quickly notice is *your deference or humble respect to a position new to you*. Irrespective of whether you're coming in as an entry level engineer or you are the new chief information officer, your job isn't to blindly start dropping the hammer on everything that looks like a nail. *Your initial steps should be to carefully observe the current state of affairs and then, only then, to look for ways to add value in moving the mission forward.*

The Greek philosopher, Epictetus, is often quoted has having said, "We have two ears and one mouth so we can listen twice as much as we speak." Now this might seem counterintuitive given the earnest desire we each have to bring success to our new team. To help tip the balance to the side of logic I offer one name: *Leroy Jenkins.*

Mr. Leroy Jenkins was a player-character in the famous online game, World Of Warcraft. As the legend goes, he joined a party of players for a big battle. As the party planned their intricate strategy, Leroy's controller-human went AFK (away from keyboard) to make a meal. He then came back, just as the party entered the big battle, oblivious of the plan they made. At that point, Leroy immediately charged headlong into battle shouting his own name, "Leroy Jenkins!" This became the now-infamous battle cry that was the trigger for his entire party being wiped out.

The moral of the story is this: You don't want your new team to wipe- so quietly collect a good amount of information and leverage the experience of your group when you start in a new position. *Truth be told, you are only successful if they are successful- and vice versa.*

Now that I've presented this general strategy, let's talk some specifics.

- Be outgoing and introduce yourself. Normally your immediate supervisor will either take you around the office to help you meet everyone or this introduction will happen in a team meeting. However, there are usually lots of people to whom you will not be formally introduced. For example, look for chances to say hello to support staff members who provide office supplies, your Quality Assurance Team, and even any internal users of the applications your new team builds. Over time you'll develop business relationships with all of these people; many of whom are non-technical. Smile, say hello to them, and engender the feeling in them that you are happy and approachable. This will help your fellow employees feel comfortable about working with and supporting you.

- Look for a seasoned pro on your team with a positive outlook. You may notice on your team a really experienced person with a crabby attitude. *Don't choose that guy.* Instead find an experienced person who shows drive and passion for the company's mission. Talk with him to get his advice on how to approach job-related tasks. Some things your boss will teach you, other things you'll be able to ask the other experienced person about. And, this kind of employee will help you navigate the company's politics.

Every company with which I've worked has had two organizational charts- the published one and the undocumented one that described how complex and difficult things actually got done. These charts were sometimes close but never the same.

The undocumented org chart is made up of the most passionate people in the company who are experts in connecting the right people at the right times in the right ways to generate the best outcomes for your clients.

Undocumented org charts skip over people in every level of the organization who attempt to hide in safe spaces- people too afraid or lazy to embrace the company mission. Your experienced, positive-thinking new friend will little by little let slip the names of these passionate people. Make note of them. This having been written, I'm not suggesting you circumvent the chain of command, however, this short list of passionate people welcome basic communication with other passionate people. And the time will come where you'll meet and have the opportunity to help them and learn from them as well. Welcome those opportunities.

- The next step in building a good foundation in your new position is to understand the expectations of the people with whom you work. The next few paragraphs focus on people at or above your level.

Every boss has a certain set of things he needs you to do consistently. This may include updating your project status every X number of days, checking in your code on a regular basis, and submitting your time card each week. These obvious ones are what people call "gimmies" or expectations very easy to meet. Print a list of these and keep them at your desk; tape this little bit of paper with them on it to your monitor if it helps. Then consistently get them done on time.

Also understand the finite list of things your boss or people above you think are taboo- bad things he doesn't want workers to do. For example, don't waste working hours surfing the internet, playing games, or goofing off on social media. This is considered slacking and you aren't being paid to slack. *When you are in the office, be completely there.*

As part of avoiding the taboo things, look to see if there are members on your team already slacking. *It's okay to be familiar with these people in ways that support your team's mission but do not hang out with them while they are slacking because you can become guilty by association.* There are two interesting and applicable proverbs to support this, "He who walks with the wise, grows wise, but a companion of fools suffers harm" and "Do not be misled: Bad company corrupts good character." This means there is risk on both ends of freely associating with slackers. First, leaders in your company will question the wisdom of your choosing to be with them and think you therefore slack with them. And secondly, the slackers will test your character by tempting you to slack with them. So tread carefully when you bump into a slacker.

If you are a boss, a mid-level manager for example, reach out to your boss and managers at your level to understand the culture of your company. Then meet with your team and help them clearly understand your list of "gimmies" with which they can effectively dispense so they can get on to the more interesting work of solving challenging problems.

Lastly, get into the habit of keeping a running to-do list of things you have done and things that need to be done.

If these are new things, talk with the right people to get them prioritized.

If these are works in progress, update their status daily so you are ready to talk about them when asked.

If these are completed items, ensure they were properly wrapped up and that you have documented any lessons you and your team learned from having worked them.

I like keeping this in a spreadsheet; to-do items on one tab and completed items with dates on the other. The to-do and done sheets also serve as a great foundation for conversations with your boss during your annual review. This long list of all the things you've accomplished can sway him when he's deciding your raise or bonus amounts and even help him justify formally promoting you to a position of more responsibility.

Going Full Cheetah

This chapter is dedicated to those engineers who have at least their first few months or even year under their belts. In the experiences to date you, the collective you, may have realized there are a next-level set of expectations your boss and company has that are unwritten. These are, in fact, the bridges of dreams connecting engineers who genuinely care about the company's mission and those managers who do too.

Once you accept and embrace your direct influence on the company's ability to create special experiences for its customers, you owe it to yourself to pursue this in *full cheetah mode-* a phrase, to my knowledge, coined by author, Seth Godin. Here I apply it directly to software engineering.

Have you seen a cheetah pursue prey? It doesn't hesitate or second guess itself- it just goes all out. Now I'm not suggesting you literally take a chunk out of anyone's hind quarter in the assertive process of doing your job. I'm suggesting you figuratively sprint and glide with the elegance of a happy cheetah- one who truly loves the opportunity before him and relentlessly leads and supports everyone towards successful outcomes. For the following set of tips, it's important to recognize the larger definition of the word "customers." Your customers might be external clients and they may well be internal teams with whom you work; the manager running your project, the QA team, or the direct users of the products you create.

- Work to create a unique interface between your customers and your company- a special relationship your customer loves. Wantonly make use of the words "please," "thank you," and "team"; in person and in email communication. *Treat everyone with whom you interact as a customer and you'll be thought of as one of those can-do people on the unwritten org chart.*

- Develop the deep domain knowledge specific to the engineering done by your team. Does your group create apps specific to a particular industry? Then dive into the deep end of that swimming pool. Learn the history of how your company has done it, how other companies are doing it, new technologies and processes for doing it, and how your clients make use of it. Come to know it inside and out and become good at talking about it utilizing the industry lingo. From there, develop some of your own thoughts and concepts. Are there some new ways to connect these systems and people? I bet there are. Become really good at what you do and get weird about it. Weird? Yes, weird!

- Look to be creative in the solutions your team provides. The mantra, "that's the way we've always done it" over time leads to large scale, inflexible processes that end up hurting the very customers they were designed to support. So always be on the lookout for new, better, and yes even seemingly weird ways to do things. Some of them won't be viable but you know what? Some of them will turn out to be spectacular. *Persistently and passionately operate with the interest of the organization foremost in your mind- and do not worry about who gets credit. People around you, above and below you in the org chart, will come to see what's truly in your heart and gravitate towards you. This is how team members evolve into leaders.*

- When you present your ideas to your boss, the diplomacy with which it is done matters. Use the words "us" and "our" and "we" a lot. As in, "Mr. Jones, given our company's challenge what do you think about us going in this direction?" Phrasing the approach in a team-oriented manner invites your boss to leverage his experience and irrespective of whether or not he goes all-in to your idea, this style demonstrates your willingness to see a bigger picture.

- Earnestly seek to take on the more complex projects available to your team. You may not always be assigned to them but do volunteer. The way one grows as an engineer is by solving interesting, challenging puzzles. And taking on complex projects serves multiple purposes. Your company needs strong technical leaders and they hired you hoping you'd eventually become one! You are going to be there for eight or more hours per day, so taking on intellectually stimulating projects is much more fun than saying nothing and ending up with the boring tasks. Also, not taking on the exciting and complex projects leaves you at the back of the pack. People who *don't try* have little upside potential and could easily be replaced. Go Full Cheetah!

- Envision yourself as that solid engineer and lead- become the next hero with Lucidchart, Jira, or the other tools of your company as well as using your mind. *Your team mates, your boss, and most importantly your myriad of customers are all looking for someone to hand them the "Easy" button, someone to help organize, lead, and tell them everything is going to be okay.* This is your special group. And, trust me, they need you- not as a dictator but as someone intellectually and happily invested in their success to the point he goes, you guessed it, *FULL CHEETAH.*

Tip: Build bridges of dreams connecting your hopes with those of your boss, your teammates, and your clients. Develop domain knowledge, incubate truly weird and creative ideas to complex problems, and step up with a sincere heart. Do these things and you'll inspire those around you to trust you with even bigger, more important things. Go Full Cheetah and you'll lay your head on your pillow each night with zero regrets and a big smile knowing you did your best.

CONCLUSION: YOUR DREAM, YOUR PATH

In the quiet moments of intellectual curiosity and day dreaming of becoming a professional engineer, you will experience delight. And organizing your unique plan to make this dream a reality is fun too. *But it only matters if you put your plan in action and commit yourself to it.*

There are many, many ways to get there- even for the least advantaged of us. Your plan might take just four years after high school or, like mine, it might take nine. If you don't have money for school, you might choose to first grow personally and experience a tour in the military service while participating in their college funding program. The mental clarity and sense of purpose one has at the end of that first four years is amazing.

Accept the truth that you must keep moving forward with your plan. Yes, slight adjustments will happen from time to time, from semester to semester. And this is normal. You may still need to work a lower-skilled job to get by while in school but you will get by. You will continue to learn, and grow even more as a person. *Just have faith and never give up.*

Transitioning from excited freshman, to determined sophomore, to committed upperclassman will give you more and more traction and motivation. Participate where it makes sense in university life, gain useful internship experience, and fully appreciate the wisdom of your professors. In this time you'll be continuing to build upon the foundation of the awesome person you will become.

In your junior and senior years, begin surveying the landscape to see where you'd like to start off; programmer, business analyst, systems analyst, or junior project manager. Each of these roles is an exciting starting point and can lead to a long-term career supporting the good mission of a company of your choosing.

Carefully select and evaluate a few companies doing work you find valuable in the world. Then follow the steps I've outlined in preparing to meet with them. Put your best foot forward and one of them will see the value you can add to their equation. Remember, in the United States as well as the rest of the world there is a true shortage of good engineers. *You will be chosen.*

Once you step foot inside your new company's large, magical kingdom, a whole new world of adventure will open up. Some parts of it will be filled with support, empathy, and awesome team play- while others will be much more challenging. How can one successfully navigate through that world? Many answers, with specific tips, are in my next book tailored to engineers who want to *power-level.*

My sincere best wishes to you in the pursuit of your dream.

Find me on Facebook @TechCoachTom for continuing real-world advice and updates!

www.ingramcontent.com/pod-product-compliance
Lightning Source LLC
LaVergne TN
LVHW042335060326
832902LV00006B/178